edexcel
advancing learning, changing lives

SPORT
AND ACTIVE LEISURE

ENTRY LEVEL
3/1

Bob Harris

Student Book

A PEARSON COMPANY

Published by Pearson Education Limited, a company incorporated in England and Wales, having its registered office at Edinburgh Gate, Harlow, Essex, CM20 2JE. Registered company number: 872828

www.pearsonschoolsandfecolleges.co.uk

Edexcel is a registered trademark of Edexcel Limited

Text © Pearson Education Limited 2010

First published 2010

13 12 11 10
10 9 8 7 6 5 4 3 2 1

British Library Cataloguing in Publication Data
A catalogue record for this book is available from the British Library.

ISBN 978 1 84690 922 1

Edited by James Croft
Designed by Pearson Education Limited
Typeset by Tek-Art
Index by Indexing Specialists (UK) Ltd
Cover design by Pearson Education Limited
Cover photo © Getty Images/Alan Thornton
Back cover photos © Shutterstock/StockLite (left), Getty Images/Adrian Green
Printed in Italy by Rotolito Lombarda

Disclaimer
This material has been published on behalf of Edexcel and offers high-quality support for the delivery of Edexcel qualifications.

This does not mean that the material is essential to achieve any Edexcel qualification, nor does it mean that this is the only suitable material available to support any Edexcel qualification. Edexcel material will not be used verbatim in setting any Edexcel examination or assessment. Any resource lists produced by Edexcel shall include this and other appropriate resources.

Copies of official specifications for all Edexcel qualifications may be found on the Edexcel website: www.edexcel.com

Contents

BTEC BTEC's own resources

About the author

Bob Harris is an experienced BTEC tutor. He has worked for over 30 years in a range of further education colleges and secondary schools, teaching both academic and vocational sports courses from Level 1 to Level 5. He is a current external verifier and has also worked as an external moderator. He has been involved in three editions of the Heinemann textbook for the BTEC First Diploma in Sport and with the BTEC Introductory Diploma in Sport and Recreation textbook.

Credits

The authors and publisher would like to thank the following individuals and organisations for permission to reproduce photographs:
The publisher would like to thank the following for their kind permission to reproduce their photographs:

(Key: b–bottom; c–centre; l–left; r–right; t–top)

Alamy Images: D. Hurst/Alamy 125, Alan Edwards/f2 Images 1, Tim Graham 135, Peter Jordan 51, LatinStock Collection 97, Dennis MacDonald 87, MasPix 38, Photofusion/David Tothill 123, Radius Images 117, Andres Rodriguez 90, Mark Wallis 17; **Corbis**: EPA/Andy Rain 15l, Erik Isakson 165, Reuters/Tim Wimbourne 8; **Getty Images**: AFP 7, AFP/Lluis Gene 84, Rodrigo Arangua 37, Bloomburg 6, Nick Clements 15tl, Dimitar Dilkoff 15r, Candice Farmer 161, Adam Gault 156, Adrian Green 103, Purcell Holmes 113, Image Source 91, Johner Images 55, Jutta Klee 169, Bryn Lennon 83, John Peters 99, Zia Soleil 107, Bob Thomas 141, Upper Cut Images 13, Darren Walsh 142; **London 2012**: 129; **Masterfile**: 89; **Pearson Education Ltd**: Comstock Images 160, Imagesource/Alamy 25, Peter Morris 159, David Sanderson 43; **Pearson Education Ltd**: Jules Selmes 105; **Press Association Images**: ABACA/Taamallah Mehdi 47, AP/Matt York 5, John Birdsall Photo Library 48, Rui Vieira 3; **Shutterstock**: 41tr, 61, Benis Arapovic 32, Yuri Arcurs 137, Yuro Arcurs 27, Atanas Bozhikov 58, Phil Date 28, 57, Mike Flippo 127, Mandy Godbehear 155, Peter Gudella 41r, Kurhan 31cr, Dean Mitchell 11, David Mzareulyan 31br, Sergey Petrov 171, StockLite 69, 71, Camilo Torres 167, Visi Stock 149

Cover images: Front: **Getty Images**: Alan Thornton; Back: **Getty Images**: Adrian Green tr; **Shutterstock**: StockLite tl

All other images © Pearson Education

About your BTEC Entry 3/Level 1 Sport and Active Leisure

Choosing to study for a BTEC Entry 3 or Level 1 Sport and Active Leisure qualification is a great decision to make for lots of reasons. Sport and active leisure continues to grow as an industry. People have more spare time and more and more activities are becoming available to them. The 2012 London Olympics should encourage even more people to be active and get involved, either by actually taking part or by helping others to do so by becoming a coach, match official or volunteer, or by supporting people in those roles. The sport industry increasingly needs people with the right skills and qualifications to support its growth.

Your BTEC Entry 3/Level 1 Sport and Active Leisure is a **vocational** or **work-related** qualification. It will give you the chance to gain knowledge, understanding and skills that are important in the subject or area of work you have chosen.

What will you be doing?

This book covers enough units for you to gain any of the following qualifications:

- BTEC Entry 3/Level 1 **Award** in Sport and Active Leisure

- BTEC Entry 3/Level 1 **Certificate** in Sport and Active Leisure

- BTEC Entry 3/Level 1 **Diploma** in Sport and Active Leisure

If you are unsure then your tutor will let you know what level of qualification you are aiming for.

How to use this book

This book is designed to help you through your BTEC Entry 3/Level 1 Sport and Active Leisure course. It is divided into 14 units to match the units in the specification. Each unit is broken down into smaller topics.

This book contains many features that will help you get the most from your course.

Introduction

Each chapter starts with a page that gives you a snapshot of what you will be learning from the unit.

TAKING PART IN SPORT **UNIT 4**

If you intend to start a career in sport and active leisure, it is important that you know about the various team and individual activities that people take part in. You need to know the rules and regulations for different sports, what clothing and equipment is required, and the skills and techniques needed to play. Knowing the basics of different sports will enable you to give simple, accurate advice to customers.

In this unit you will learn:

- How to take part in team sports
- How to take part in individual sports
- To look at your performance and say what went well and what could be improved

What does it mean to be a team player?

Activities

You will find activities throughout the book. These will help you understand the information in the unit and give you a chance to try things for yourself.

Activity: Different strokes

What different techniques do you use in your chosen sport? Why do you need different techniques? Describe the different situations in which you might use them.

Case studies

Case studies show you how what you are learning about applies in the real world of work.

Case study:
Healthy eating event

Laura has just helped at a Healthy Eating event, where people were given information on how to improve their diet. Laura assisted at the event by supervising visitor parking. Laura was late for one of the briefings and missed the part where assistants were told of another event happening at the same time. It was decided that the car park should be split into two areas. It was stressed how important it was that people were directed to the correct parking area. Laura also failed to listen to what she was told by another team member. She did not understand where parking for the Healthy Eating event was. On the day, she forgot her high visibility jacket and ID pass. When a visitor complained about how difficult it was to park, Laura could not be found.

Functional skills

Useful pointers showing you where you can improve your skills in English, mathematics and ICT.

Functional skills

Keeping a performance diary will help develop your writing and improve your skills in English.

Key terms

The words you need to understand are easy to spot, and their meanings are clearly explained.

✳ Key term

Sport
An activity that involves physical exertion and competition.

Remember!

Look out for these boxes. They point out really important information.

❗ Remember

Taking part in dance workshops will help you improve a range of skills.

Check

You'll find a reminder of key information at the end of each topic.

✔ Check

- Playing sport involves working with others to achieve a result
- All sports require specialist clothing, either for safety, visibility, ease of movement or to identify which team you are playing for.

Assessment page

This page will help you check what you have done so far and give you tips for getting the best grade you can for each task.

Assessment overview

This table shows you what assessment criteria you need to meet to pass the unit, and on which pages you will find activities and information to help you prepare for your assignments.

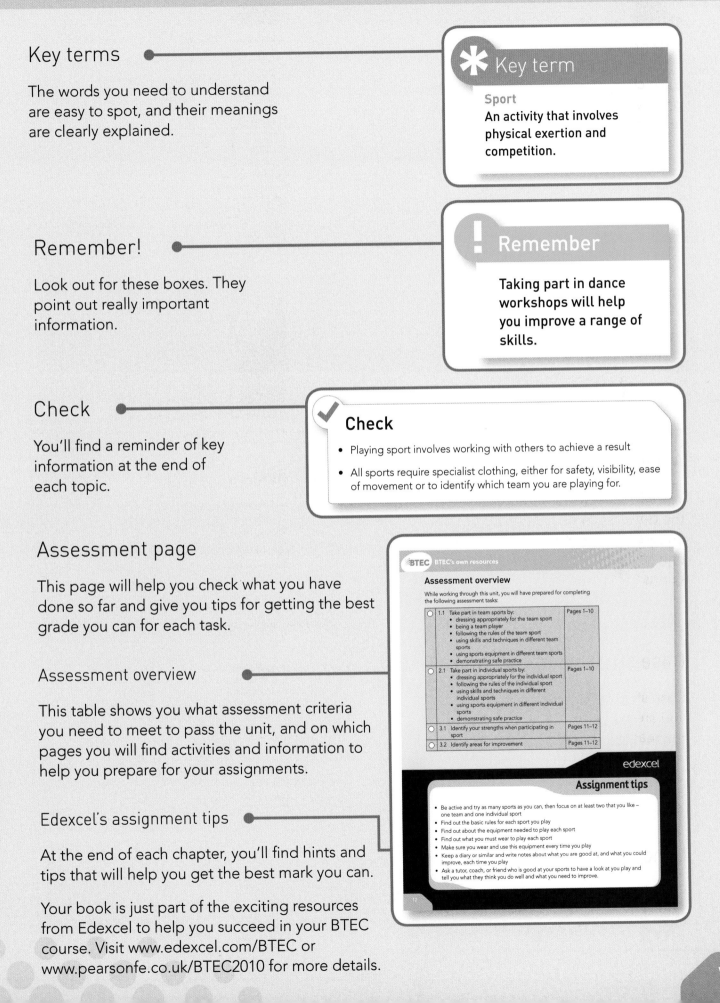

BTEC BTEC's own resources

Assessment overview

While working through this unit, you will have prepared for completing the following assessment tasks:

○	1.1	Take part in team sports by: • dressing appropriately for the team sport • being a team player • following the rules of the team sport • using skills and techniques in different team sports • using sports equipment in different team sports • demonstrating safe practice	Pages 1–10
○	2.1	Take part in individual sports by: • dressing appropriately for the individual sport • following the rules of the individual sport • using skills and techniques in different individual sports • using sports equipment in different individual sports • demonstrating safe practice	Pages 1–10
○	3.1	Identify your strengths when participating in sport	Pages 11–12
○	3.2	Identify areas for improvement	Pages 11–12

edexcel

Assignment tips

- Be active and try as many sports as you can, then focus on at least two that you like – one team and one individual sport
- Find out the basic rules for each sport you play
- Find out about the equipment needed to play each sport
- Find out what you must wear to play each sport
- Make sure you wear and use this equipment every time you play
- Keep a diary or similar and write notes about what you are good at, and what you could improve, each time you play
- Ask a tutor, coach, or friend who is good at your sports to have a look at you play and tell you what they think you do well and what you need to improve.

Edexcel's assignment tips

At the end of each chapter, you'll find hints and tips that will help you get the best mark you can.

Your book is just part of the exciting resources from Edexcel to help you succeed in your BTEC course. Visit www.edexcel.com/BTEC or www.pearsonfe.co.uk/BTEC2010 for more details.

TAKING PART IN SPORT

UNIT 4

If you intend to start a career in sport and active leisure, it is important that you know about the various team and individual activities that people take part in. You need to know the rules and regulations for different sports, what clothing and equipment is required, and the skills and techniques needed to play. Knowing the basics of different sports will enable you to give simple, accurate advice to customers.

In this unit you will learn:

- How to take part in team sports

- How to take part in individual sports

- To look at your performance and say what went well and what could be improved

What does it mean to be a team player?

L01 Taking part in team &
L02 individual sports

There are now a wide range of team and individual **sports** on offer. They may take place indoors or outdoors, in the summer or in the winter.

Some sports, such as golf, are target games. Some, like rounders, involve a 'bat and ball'. Some involve a net (volleyball), while others are striking games (cricket). Some games, such as rugby, involve physical contact, while others, like netball, do not. Others take place in or on the water. They may involve powered craft or, like sailing, they may rely on the wind. Some sports, such as badminton or squash, take place in purpose-built facilities, while others, such as climbing, canoeing and orienteering, take place out in the countryside.

Can you think of other examples?

> **✳ Key term**
>
> **Sport**
> An activity that involves physical exertion and competition.

◎ Activity: Pair work

In pairs, list as many different team and individual sports as you can.

Being a team player

Being in a team means that you need to be a *team player*. But what does this mean? It might mean helping the rest of your team mates to achieve a shared goal, like trying to score as many runs as possible in a cricket match. It might mean using your skills and techniques to help a team mate be successful. In the Tour de France, for example, a cyclist may ride *for* a team mate to try to ensure that he is first over the finish line. In some sports, like athletics for example, you compete as an individual but are still part of a team.

Being a team player also means respecting your team mates and giving them your full support. It means trying your best at all times, even if you are having a bad game.

Activity: Sports you play

Think about the sports you currently play either at school or college or in your own time. For each sport, make a poster identifying:

- What the sport involves
- The rules of the game
- Any equipment that is required
- What you need to wear and why
- How you support other team mates.

Think about the need for each item of clothing you have listed. Is it for safety, for ease of movement or to distinguish you from other players?

✔ Check

- Playing sport involves working with others to achieve a result
- All sports require specialist clothing, either for safety, visibility, ease of movement or to identify which team you are playing for.

L01
L02
Sports skills & techniques

To play sport, you must be able to perform a range of **skills** and **techniques**. Skills in sport are *abilities* that have to be learned and require teaching or coaching. Techniques are the *way* we perform or apply a skill.

The diagram below shows a variety of skills required for different team sports.

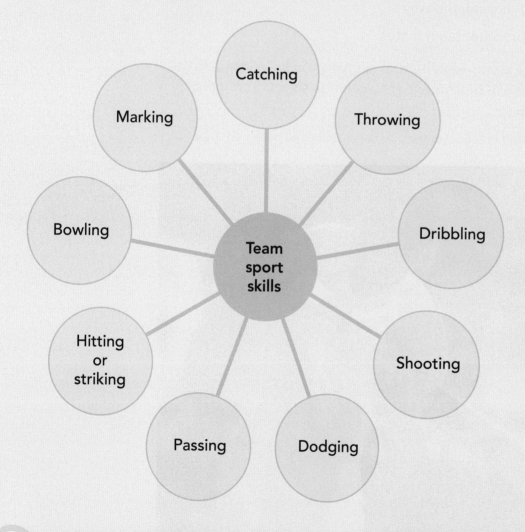

◎ Activity: Team sport skills

Think of a team sport that you play. Which of the skills shown in the diagram are required for your sport? Now compare with a partner. What skills are common to both of your sports? Are there skills that are specific to your sport? Why is this?

Different techniques

The same skill can usually be performed or applied in a number of different ways. A footballer might use either their left or right foot when kicking the ball. When taking a penalty, they may take more or fewer steps than their team mate.

Often the choice of technique that a sportsperson employs depends on the opponent. Imagine playing against a left-handed and then a right-handed batsman in a cricket match. If you were the bowler, you would try to place the ball in a different position on the wicket in order to get each one out.

Different techniques are required to overcome various obstacles and challenges that occur in sport. A golfer needs a range of different techniques, and clubs, for striking the ball depending on where and how it lies, on or off the fairway.

Different techniques are required when the weather is bad, or the conditions are poor. For example, a tennis player may use different shots and patterns of movement when playing in high winds. A rugby player may use a different technique when taking a penalty kick if the pitch is very wet.

Activity: Different strokes

What different techniques do you use in your chosen sport? Why do you need different techniques? Describe the different situations in which you might use them.

✔ Check

- Skills are abilities that are learned
- Techniques are the way we perform or apply skills
- The sports we play require a range of skills and techniques.

L01 L02 Rules for sport

When playing a sport, we have to follow a set of rules and regulations, and a set scoring system, if we are to win the game. **Rules** cover:

- The number of players per side
- The length of a match
- What a player can and cannot do
- What a player must wear.

Some rules are for the safety of players and spectators.

Regulations generally apply to the equipment that is used in a game, the size of the pitch or court, and how matches or tournaments should be run.

In table tennis, for example, the regulations state that the racket can be any size, shape or weight, but the blade needs to be flat and rigid. This means that your racket can be any size you want, but the larger it is, the more difficult it will be to use. In practice, most rackets are 15 cm wide and 25 cm long, including the handle.

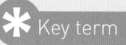

Key term

Rules
Tell us what we can and cannot do in sport.

Functional skills

Reading and understanding rules will help you develop your skills in **English**.

Case study:

Record-breaking swimwear

There was great controversy at the Beijing Olympic Games in 2008 when many swimmers broke records wearing form-fitting swimsuits constructed from specially engineered fabrics to reduce water resistance.

A total of 66 Olympic records were broken at the Games; 70 world records were broken that year. In one race the first five finishers had world record-beating times.

As of 1 January 2010, the rules of the sport have been changed. Although use of the fabric itself has not been banned, men are now only permitted to wear suits from the waist to above the knees, and they may only wear one piece of swimwear.

Activity: A beginner's guide

For one of the sports you play, write a simple guide to the basic rules for a beginner. Start by explaining the object of the game. Include examples to help you explain the rules.

Check

- Rules and regulations tell us what we can and cannot do when playing a sport

- Rules and regulations apply to what players wear and the equipment they may use

- Rules make sure that, wherever and with whoever you play a sport, it will be played in the same way.

L01 L02 Equipment needed for sport

Equipment is needed for almost all sports. Some sports require a wide range of equipment. You may need:

- Flags to mark the pitch, showing where the boundaries are
- Nets for the goal, to catch the ball, or to throw into to score a basket
- Posts to support nets
- Bats, rackets or sticks to strike a ball, puck or shuttle
- Balls, pucks or shuttles
- A score board, screen or display so that players and spectators can see the score.

Can you think of other items of equipment needed for sports? What about sports not played on a pitch?

Equipment may be required for safety reasons. For example, rugby goal posts are often padded to protect a player if they hit the posts during a game.

Activity: Equipped for the game

Think about the following very different sports: canoeing, hockey and tennis. List the equipment needed to:

- Take part as a player
- Make the game safe for players
- Mark the playing area.

As we have seen, rules and regulations also apply to the equipment used in sports. They cover:

- The size of any equipment
- What it can be made from
- The form it can take.

Activity: Sports bag

Think about one team and one individual sport that you enjoy. List the equipment you need to play a match or game, including any personal equipment you use. Take photographs showing these items of equipment being used. What is each item for? What basic rules are there about each item of equipment?

Functional skills

Listing the equipment you need for a sports activity will help you develop your writing skills in English.

Activity: Formula One racing

Visit the Formula One website and look at how many rules apply to the cars used. Why do you think this is?

✔ Check

- There are rules covering the shape and size of any sports equipment and what it is made of
- Rules make sure that the equipment used is the same for everyone who plays
- Rules make sure that games are fair and safe.

L03 Reviewing your performance in sport

Reviewing your performance is important if you want to improve as a player.

When you review your performance, you should try to identify what could be better and think about how to change it to improve.

Your review might look like this:

| Not able to perform a skill successfully | Look at the skill using video analysis or a coach | Look for weaknesses in the skill and their causes | Work on the weaknesses seen to improve them | Watch the skill again to see if it has improved |

When you review your sports performance, you need to look at both your performance as an individual player and as part of a team. When observing your team activities, do you look at the performance of the team as a whole or just your own performance? Do you tend to focus on one skill or a whole range of skills? What about the techniques that you use? It may be that in certain playing conditions, you need to develop a better technique to help you be successful.

Your review will help you identify your areas of weakness and steps you need to take to correct them.

Observation and analysis

Your review might consist of the following stages of observation and analysis:

- A match observation
- A skills test that you are required to perform
- A video analysis
- A discussion with an experienced coach, your PE tutor or instructor.

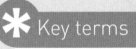
Key term

Reviewing
Looking back on something to decide what was good and what needs improving.

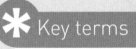
Key terms

Observation
When you watch the way someone does something closely and take notes as part of a review.

Analysis
When you talk someone through how they performed to point out what went well and what could be improved.

Activity: Performance review

Conduct a simple performance review with a partner. You can record each other's performance with a digital camera or camcorder for later analysis, or make notes or keep a tally chart. Record your review in a suitable format, such as a simple table to show the results of your review, with a written description of what was observed.

Functional skills

Writing a review will help you develop your skills in English.

Case study:

Badminton skills review

Roy Baker plays badminton every Monday evening at a local badminton club. One of his coaches has written the following review report and given it to Roy.

I watched Roy play badminton and observed the following:

Roy has a good serve, both short and long. He successfully won 10 points in the match directly from his serve. His short serve was his best causing his opponent to lift the shuttle high into the air, which allowed Roy to hit a smash and win the point. Roy did not use a long serve very often. When he did, it was often too short, allowing his opponent to attack Roy and force errors.

Roy has good footwork. He is quick around the court and is always balanced when he plays a shot. Roy uses mostly forehand shots. His backhand is very weak and he makes many mistakes as a result.

Activity: Room for improvement

What are Roy's strengths? What are the areas of his game he needs to work on? Why?

Check

- Reviewing your performance is important if you want to get better
- There are many ways to review your performance but they all involve observation and analysis
- Choose the right method for you based on what you want to review and the facilities available.

ASSESSMENT OVERVIEW

While working through this unit, you will have prepared for completing the following assessment tasks:

○	1.1	Take part in team sports by: • dressing appropriately for the team sport • being a team player • following the rules of the team sport • using skills and techniques in different team sports • using sports equipment in different team sports • demonstrating safe practice	Pages 2–9
○	2.1	Take part in individual sports by: • dressing appropriately for the individual sport • following the rules of the individual sport • using skills and techniques in different individual sports • using sports equipment in different individual sports • demonstrating safe practice	Pages 2–9
○	3.1	Identify your strengths when participating in sport	Pages 10–11
○	3.2	Identify areas for improvement	Pages 10–11

edexcel :::

Assignment tips

- Be active and try as many sports as you can, then focus on at least two that you like – one team and one individual sport
- Find out the basic rules for each sport you play
- Find out about the equipment needed to play each sport
- Find out what you must wear to play each sport
- Make sure you wear and use this equipment every time you play
- Keep a diary or similar and write notes about what you are good at, and what you could improve, each time you play
- Ask a tutor, coach, or friend who is good at your sports, to have a look at you play and tell you what they think you do well and what you need to improve.

ASSISTING AT A SPORT OR ACTIVE LEISURE EVENT

To assist at sport and active leisure events, you need to know the difference between competition events and leisure-based events, and what they require from those involved in helping at the event.

Sport and active leisure events take place at local, regional and national level. Sports events range from local football tournaments to national athletics meets. Active leisure events include sponsored walks or swims and charity fun runs.

In this unit you will learn:

- About different types of active leisure and sport events

- How to help at an active leisure or sport event

- To look at your performance and say what went well and what could be improved

What qualities do you think are important in someone helping at a sport or active leisure event?

13

L01 Types of active leisure & sport events

You need to understand the difference between Sports events and Active leisure events.

Sports events are competitive, have rules and regulations and produce a winner. They range from large-scale events like FA Cup or Premier League matches to much smaller local events such as a school sports fixture or local netball tournament.

Active leisure events are concerned with *non*-competitive activities. For example, sponsored activities like a 'Race for Life' fun run raise money for cancer research. See the Race for Life website for more information.

Aims and goals

People take part in sport and active leisure events for all sorts of reasons:

- For the excitement of competition
- To be the best that they can at their sport
- To be the best in the world
- To have a go at something new
- To improve their health
- To raise awareness for a cause
- To raise money for charity.

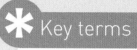

Key terms

Active leisure events
Active leisure events are concerned with non-competitive activities, such as fun runs and charity events.

Sports events
Sports events are competitive, have rules and regulations, and produce a winner.

Activity: What motivates you?

Which of these reasons apply only to charity events? Which apply only to sports events? Can you think of any other reasons why people might want to take part in sport or active leisure events? What motivates you to take part?

Activity: Recognising different types of events

Look at these images. How would you describe the differences between each of the events pictured?

Different sport and active leisure activities may be organised by local teams or groups or by national or international organisations. Whoever organises these events, people are needed who are willing and able to assist with the organisation and running of the event – people like you.

Check

- Active leisure events are where people take part for fun or to raise money for a good cause. They may involve people of all ages and backgrounds.

- Sports events are competitive and involve games with set rules and regulations, such as football or tennis. They may involve only men, women or people of a particular age group, so that the competition is fair.

LO1 Getting ready to help at an event

All events require planning and organisation and this requires certain skills and abilities of the people who assist.

To assist at an event, you need to show good **self-management**.

This involves:

- Planning and doing things at the right time
- Clear communication with people who need to know things
- Always showing professional behaviour and positive attitudes
- Working well as part of a team.

When assisting at an event, you must:

- Wear the right clothes, etc for the event or time of year
- Plan what you have to do, where you are supposed to be and when, and make sure you are there on time.

Key term

Self-management
Organising yourself for an event.

Activity: The right clothes

Often a car parking assistant will wear a high visibility jacket. Why is this item of clothing important? What else might they need to wear if the event were held in the winter, or at night?

Case study:

Winter fun run for charity

Stephanie is assisting with a local fun run in December to raise money for a local animal sanctuary. She has been asked to be a marshal directing runners. The event starts at 10 am on Sunday morning. The course follows some busy local main roads, as well as using local lanes and the local park. Some local celebrities have entered and large numbers of spectators are expected. Among the many other participants are both experienced and inexperienced runners, some of them running to try to beat their personal best times, and others to raise money for different charities. Runners are expected to be out on the course for some time, possibly for longer than the set time for which the roads are closed. Once this set time has passed, traffic will be allowed to use the roads again as normal.

Activity: 'To do' list

Make a list of what Stephanie needs to do to make sure she is successful in her self-management. Describe how she should dress. Draw up a brief timetable for her day to make sure she completes everything she needs to do successfully.

Check

- Make sure you are properly dressed, on time and you know where you should be

- Always complete the tasks you are given.

L01 Using your time & communicating well

Good communication and time-keeping are some of the most important skills that an event assistant requires.

Good time-keeping

You need to make sure that you are always on time and that you complete any jobs in the time allowed. You may have to attend a planning meeting before an event. If you are late, the meeting may start without you. If it cannot start until you are there, you will have made everyone, including yourself, late for whatever might follow after the meeting.

Imagine the starter for the London Marathon being half an hour late for the start of the race!

Good communication

Communication involves giving and receiving information.

At an event you *give* information mainly by speaking or writing.

You *receive* information by listening to instructions and making sure that you understand them so you can follow them correctly.

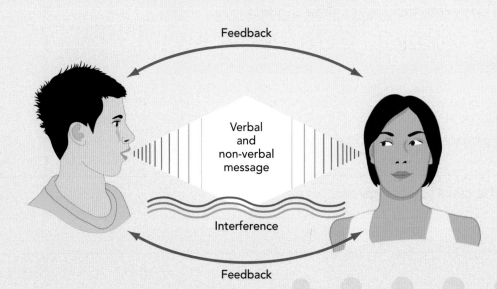

Feedback

Verbal and non-verbal message

Interference

Feedback

The diagram shows two people communicating. Feedback means giving information which checks understanding. The receiver might repeat instructions to show they understand. Interference stops the receiver understanding correctly. You might also have to share information with others in a team or with members of the public who are taking part in your event.

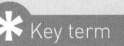

Key term

Feedback
Information you give that shows you understand or that an agreed aim or goal has been met.

Activity: Message received and understood

You have already made a list of what Stephanie needs to do to prepare and self-manage for the fun run. Now make a list or poster with a partner showing how she can make sure that she listens to and follows instructions she is given about what she needs to do and when. How can she make sure that tasks are completed effectively, as and when they are required? Why is this important to the event and for Stephanie?

Functional skills

Discussing things and sharing information with others will help you develop your skills in English.

Check

- Always be on time

- Make sure that you complete tasks in the time allowed

- Make sure that you communicate clearly, repeat instructions and check that you understand.

L02 Helping at an event

When assisting at an event, the right attitude and behaviour are important.

Imagine helping at a fun day for young children. As an assistant, parents would expect you to behave responsibly, to know what you are doing and to be confident with young children. It might be especially important to the children themselves that you are friendly and like to laugh and have fun, but they also need to feel that you have clear and firm boundaries.

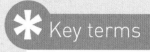

Key terms

Attitude
Our way of thinking about something.

Behaviour
The way we act.

Activity: The right attitude

Imagine you are an assistant to a team of sports leaders who are running an adult sports session. What attitudes and behaviours would you expect them to show?

Motivation

A leader or assistant at an event who shows motivation looks and acts like they want to be there. They keep the purpose of the event clearly in focus at all times. They encourage people participating to do their best, make sure that they are enjoying themselves and have the best interests of those participating at heart.

Enthusiasm

Enthusiastic leaders and assistants show real enjoyment of what they are doing. They smile. They are positive and encouraging. They help to make activities and events fun for everyone taking part. They don't show anger or lose their temper.

Key term

Enthusiastic
Being really keen on something.

Showing initiative

Showing initiative means not waiting to be told to do something when you can see that something needs doing. For example, an event assistant should not wait to be told to deal with a lost or injured child. They should act immediately *on their own initiative*.

Activity: Positive attitude

In small groups, discuss PE tutors or instructors you know. Do they show these positive attitudes? How do these attitudes affect the sessions they lead?

Being a team player

It is important also to act as a member of a team. Sport and active leisure events cannot be organised by one person – large events often need many people to organise and assist. Setting up equipment needs a group of people to work together if the job is to be done quickly and safely. For an event to be run successfully everyone needs to play their part.

Activity: Showing initiative as an assistant

What attitudes and behaviours should Stephanie show when assisting at the fun run? Why are they important? Think of ways Stephanie could show initiative when assisting. Why might this be important?

Check

- Be motivated, show you want to be there and that the event is important to you

- Be enthusiastic and encouraging at all times

- Be ready and willing to act when you need to, without being told.

L02 Checking your performance

At the end of any event, it is important that you look back at how you performed. You should think about:

- The skills you used

- The techniques you used

- What areas of your performance need to be better.

Remember, skills are abilities that we have to learn, such as how to communicate by speaking and listening. Techniques refer to how we perform or apply a skill. For example, we might communicate in writing, on the telephone or by email.

Why review your performance?

It may be that the way we received instructions for an event resulted in something going wrong. For example, the instructions may have been too detailed to be given over the phone and you did not check your notes and give feedback.

Looking at how well you did will help you to know what you need to improve so that at the next event you assist with, you will perform better. This will mean that:

- Participants and spectators will enjoy themselves more

- The event will be more successful

- You will enjoy yourself more, which will make you even more enthusiastic and motivated.

How to review your performance

You might review your own performance at an event in a number of ways:

- Meet with a supervisor to discuss your performance

- Watch a video of your performance

- Ask participants and/or spectators to complete a feedback sheet

- Keep a diary of your assistance with events and self-assess your performance

- Ask other team members how you did.

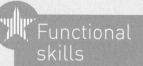
Functional skills

Keeping a performance diary will help develop your writing and improve your skills in English.

Once you know what you need to be better at, you can practise skills or techniques to make them better.

Case study:
Healthy eating event

Laura has just helped at a Healthy Eating event, where people were given information on how to improve their diet. Laura assisted at the event by supervising visitor parking. Laura was late for one of the briefings and missed the part where assistants were told of another event happening at the same time. It was decided that the car park should be split into two areas. It was stressed how important it was that people were directed to the correct parking area. Laura also failed to listen to what she was told by another team member. She did not understand where parking for the Healthy Eating event was. On the day, she forgot her high visibility jacket and ID pass. When a visitor complained about how difficult it was to park, Laura could not be found.

Activity: Pair work

In pairs, discuss what Laura needs to improve. What would be the benefits, to both Laura and the event, of improving Laura's performance?

Check

- Reviewing your performance tells you what you need to do better

- There are many ways to review your performance

- Try keeping a diary of your assistance with events to check how you are getting on.

ASSESSMENT OVERVIEW

While working through this unit, you will have prepared for completing the following assessment tasks:

◯	1.1	Identify active leisure events	Pages 14–15
◯	1.2	Identify sport events	Pages 14–15
◯	1.3	Identify ways to assist at an event	Pages 16–17
◯	2.1	Assist at an active leisure or sport event by: • dressing appropriately for the event • being an active and positive member of the team throughout the event • listening to and following instructions accurately	Pages 18–21
◯	2.2	Review your strengths in assisting at a sports or active leisure event, in terms of: • your appearance • your contribution to the team • your accuracy in following instructions	Pages 22–23

edexcel

Assignment tips

- Look at a number of different events, local, regional and national

- When assisting at an event, make sure you take an *active* part and show what you can do. Make a checklist of what you need to wear, what you need to take with you, and what time you need to be there. Remember to listen carefully to instructions and repeat them to show you understand.

- Keep a diary or notebook to record all the jobs you carry out at events. Get your tutor or other event leader to sign your diary or notebook to confirm what you did at the event. Ask them to comment on how well you performed in your role. Using this feedback, you can then make a list of areas where you need to do better and think about the benefits of improving your performance.

IMPROVING OWN FITNESS

People today are more aware of their health and fitness than ever before. Over the past ten or twenty years, there has been a huge increase in the number of fitness suites and health studios. There is now a wide range of exercise and fitness classes available for people who want to improve their own level of fitness.

You need to participate actively in different exercise and fitness sessions in order to develop an understanding of what each type of exercise involves. You need to learn and follow the correct dress code for exercising, show you can follow instructions and be aware of health and safety considerations.

In this unit you will learn:

- About different exercise and fitness activities

- Skills for work, including how to manage your time, dress appropriately for exercise, and follow an activity leader's instructions

- How to follow health and safety guidelines

- To look at your performance and say what went well and what could be improved

What motivates you to exercise?

LO1 Know about different exercise &
LO2 fitness activities

People have different fitness requirements and enjoy different activities when it comes to **exercising**. The modern fitness industry tries to provide a range of opportunities to help anyone who wants to get and stay fit. These include the facilities provided at large, purpose-built fitness clubs, as well as those taking place at small local village halls.

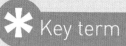

✻ Key term

Exercise (exercising)
The activity of making use of your muscles in various ways to keep fit.

Indoor and outdoor activities

Exercise and fitness activities can take place either indoors or outdoors.

Activity: Indoor activities for all weathers

With a partner, make a list of indoor activities that are regarded as 'exercise and fitness' activities. How many different activities can you think of?

Indoor activities include common energetic exercise activities such as fitness classes, aerobics, and swimming, as well as less 'traditional' activities such as pilates, yoga, body combat or boxercise. Even ice skating and bowls are exercise activities for many people.

Outdoor exercise includes a wide range of activities, from energetic sports such as tennis and football, to less strenuous activities such as walking or jogging. Exercise activities may be done on your own or in groups.

With both indoor and outdoor activities, a variety of factors such as age, income, availability of facilities and the time a person has available will all influence the type of activity a person chooses to take part in.

Activity: The right exercise activity for your needs

Choose two different fitness activities – one indoor and one outdoor. Once you have taken part in both, write down what you liked and disliked about each one and why. How well did the different activities suit your fitness and other needs?

How well would each activity suit a person:

- with limited money?
- who is new to exercise?
- who is experienced at taking exercise?

Give reasons for your answers, using examples where possible.

✓ Check

- Exercise can be taken indoors and outdoors
- You can exercise on your own or in a group or class
- There are activities to suit everyone.

L01 Gathering information

People who are thinking about starting some form of exercise need access to information about what activities, facilities and classes are available.

It is important that information about these activities is easy to find, gives all the necessary information and is available in the right places. Otherwise people will not be able to find out what they need to know to attend the classes.

Activities are publicised in a variety of ways. Organisers often use more than one way of telling people about what they have to offer. These include:

- The Yellow Pages
- Local newspapers
- Word of mouth
- Posters or leaflets in doctors' surgeries
- Radio
- Internet
- Posters on community noticeboards.

Functional skills

Reading through this type of information will help you improve your skills in English.

Case study:

New in town

Parveen has just moved to a new town. He is keen to take part in some fitness activity locally. He is not sure what is available and doesn't know many people yet who could help him. He finds out about three local providers from The Yellow Pages and decides to call them up to ask about the fitness activities they offer. He asks them quite a few questions on the telephone, has them send him information in the post, and then visits their websites to get as much information as he possibly can. He even hears an advert for one of the fitness centres on his list on the radio. In the end Parveen decides that the provider with the best website is the right one for him, because he can get regular and convenient updates on the services he wants to use.

Activity: Publicity poster

Choose *three* sources of information about both indoor and outdoor exercise activities available where you live. Present the information you have gathered in the form of a poster for a local leisure centre, doctor's surgery, shop window or community noticeboard to inform local people about these activities. Remember to think about what information a person would need to know about the activities before you begin making your poster.

Activity: Choosing the right way to communicate

Using the internet is a good way of telling people about local services. However, not everyone has a computer.

How many of your older relatives have internet access? Do they know how to use it? What would be a better way to tell older people about exercise and fitness activities they might like to take part in?

If you wanted to advertise exercise classes aimed at new mothers, how and where would you do this and why?

Check

- If people are to be active, they need to know what is available, where and when

- There are many ways of finding out information about exercise and fitness activities

- It is always good to use more than one way of sharing the information people need.

L02 Active participation in exercise & fitness activities

Being an active participant means that you actually take part in fitness activities on a regular basis.

When you take part in exercise and fitness activities, many of the qualities that you will need to succeed are also needed and expected by people you work with.

Enthusiasm

Being enthusiastic about taking part helps you to enjoy the activity you have chosen and put in the necessary effort, which is important if you are going to improve your health and fitness.

If you lack enthusiasm for what you are doing, this will affect the effort you make and you will be more likely to give it up.

At work, your employer will expect you to be enthusiastic about your job and working for the organisation.

Motivation

Being motivated is also an important factor. People who are motivated keep the reasons why they are taking part clearly in focus at all times. If you are going to take part in regular exercise, you must be able to answer the question 'Why?'

People exercise for a variety of reasons. They may want to:

- Lose weight

- Prepare for a specific event, like a half marathon for example

- Recover from an illness, such as a heart problem.

Some people exercise simply because they enjoy it, but most people need to have something to aim for. Again, if you do not have a reason to exercise, you are more likely to give it up.

Activity: Trying something new

There is a wide range of exercise activities available. It is important to be open minded and willing to try different activities. Some people take part in an exercise activity simply to try something new. Is there a sport you have not tried before? Have a go. What did you like about the activity and what did you dislike? Be as positive as you can.

Body language

When you take part in any exercise activity, you communicate a lot to people without actually saying anything. You do this through your body language.

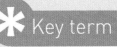

Key term

Body language
Movements or positions of your body that let other people know what you are thinking or feeling.

Activity: Positive and negative body language

Look at the two images on the right. Which person shows *positive* body language? Why?

Having a *positive attitude* is important when exercising. Believing the exercise you are doing is having a positive benefit is key. Think about completing course work for this course. If you do not think it is important, how do you think you will do?

Activity: Reading body language

Spend some time observing people in your centre going about their daily life. Can you 'read' their body language? What is it saying?

✓ Check

- Be enthusiastic and motivated about what you are doing

- Be open minded and try a wide range of activities

- Have a positive attitude and think what your body is saying to others.

LO2 Managing your time, appearance & safety

Using your time well

When you are given a task, do you usually complete it in the time available? If not, why not? Is it because you waste time or do you put things off until another time?

In exercise activities, good time-keeping means arriving on time for a class or exercise session and being ready to start as soon as you arrive. The same will be required of you at work. Your employer will expect you to be on time and to complete tasks in the time you have been given.

Being serious about taking exercise will teach you the same skills you will need if you are going to be serious about your career.

Dress code

If you taking exercise regularly, you are required to adopt the right dress code. In other words, you need to dress appropriately for the activity. For most exercise activities it is important that your clothes fit well and allow you to move freely. If you look the part, it will help you have a positive attitude and communicate to others that you are serious about what you are doing. Wearing the right clothing also helps prevent accidents and injuries.

Activity: Dressed for fitness

Look at the image on the right. How are the fitness instructor and the client dressed? What does this say about them and their attitude? How will the way they are dressed affect the way they work together?

Health and safety

It is important to think about both your own and others' health and safety. If you think about health and safety when you exercise, you will understand its importance at work.

There are a number of laws which give employers, employees and clients important responsibilities when it comes to health and safety.

Activity: Preventing injury

Look at the image of the fitness instructor and the client exercising again. What health and safety points might the exercise professional be advising the client about?

Activity: Following instructions

Consider the following situations. With a partner, discuss what might happen because the client has failed to act as advised. What problems might arise? What accidents might happen? Who might be hurt as a result?

1. The instructor shows the client and explains in detail how to use a piece of equipment. The client thinks they know better, does not listen and uses the piece of equipment in a completely different way.

2. The client does not bother to wipe down each piece of equipment they use with a clean towel before the next person uses it.

3. The client wears inappropriate clothing that does not fit well and also wears jewellery which he has been told is not allowed.

Check

- Manage your time well
- Look smart and dress for the activity
- Always follow instructions exactly and think 'safety first' at all times.

L03 Reviewing your performance

Whether you are exercising or at work, you never stop learning and developing. It is important that you review your performance to find out what can be improved and which skills need to be developed further. By identifying your strengths and weaknesses, you will know *what* and *how* to improve.

We can review our performance as follows:

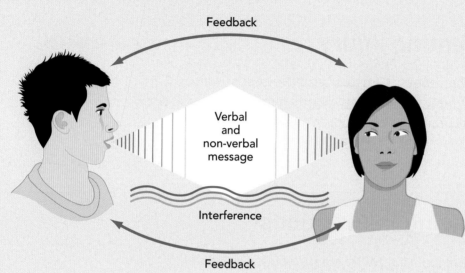

Peer assessment

Peer assessment involves people you work with, whether you are exercising or at work, giving feedback about how you are doing. It is important that both you and the person you are working with are happy with this arrangement and that you trust each other to be honest and fair.

Self-assessment

Self-assessment is where *you assess your own performance*. This is where you 'take a step back' and 'look in the mirror'. Again, it is important that you are honest with yourself if your feedback is to be of value.

Employer appraisal

At work, your supervisor – the person who is responsible for you – may provide feedback or an appraisal of your work. This may be written or spoken. Taking a video recording is another way of reviewing performance. It enables you, and others, to watch how a task or activity was performed and then say what was good and bad. Your fitness instructor might video you performing a particular exercise to show you where you can improve your technique. At work, it might be used to analyse you lifting a heavy object safely or dealing with difficult customers.

Key term

Appraisal
Judging how good something is.

Activity: Recording for staff training purposes

Many firms record telephone conversations between customers and staff for staff training purposes. How might recording a telephone conversation help a telesales member of staff to improve their performance?

Questionnaires

Questionnaires are another way to review performance. They can be filled in by a staff member, a supervisor or by clients/customers. Once results have been gathered, organisations can analyse the findings to improve staff performance. This will improve the performance of the whole organisation. In an exercise setting, the instructor might ask the client to answer questions about the programme they have been following, how effective it has been and what the client has enjoyed or disliked. This helps the instructor to improve or develop the programme for the good of the client.

Activity: Practise self-assessment

Choose two different exercise activities and two different fitness classes or sessions you would like to take part in. For each of these activities and sessions, show that you can:

- Dress appropriately
- Follow instructions given to you
- Follow health and safety guidance
- Show suitable time-keeping ability, arriving on time, being ready to take part, etc.

After each activity or session, take a step back and make notes on how you think you perfomed in each of these areas.

Checking

- Review your performance regularly
- Be honest with yourself
- Identify what you need to do better.

ASSESSMENT OVERVIEW

While working through this unit, you will have prepared for completing the following assessment tasks:

○	1.1	Identify different exercise and fitness activities	Pages 26–29
○	2.1	Actively participate in exercise and fitness activities and demonstrate: • time management skills • appropriate dress for the activity • following instructions provided by the activity leader • following health and safety guidelines before, during and after activities	Pages 30–33
○	3.1	Identify your strengths and areas for improvement in exercise and fitness activities	Pages 34–36

edexcel

Assignment tips

- Find out what exercise and fitness activities are available at school or college and locally

- Choose *two* exercise activities and *two* fitness activities and take part in at least one of each

- When taking part make sure you wear the right clothing and footwear

- Show that you are able to follow instructions given by a fitness instructor during a class or exercise session

- Keep a diary or make notes on what you have completed, what you were good at, and what you need to improve

- Get an instructor or your tutor to sign your diary or notes to confirm what you have done.

MANAGING YOUR HEALTH AT WORK

Different places of work present different health and safety risks. Whatever your place of work, being at work can affect you both physically and mentally. While at work, you might experience a minor strain to your back or a headache, or you might develop a more serious long-term problem such as Repetitive Strain Injury (RSI). Being able to recognise possible risks to your health while at work will help you take steps to protect yourself. By staying healthy, your work will be more enjoyable, and you will be more productive and effective.

In this unit you will learn:

- That different areas of work have different health needs

- How to keep healthy in different work areas

Why might an awareness of health risks be especially important for people working in sport or active leisure?

L01 Different places of work

There are a number of different places of work, all of which present different health and safety risks.

Type of work	Workplace
Sport and active leisure	Sports centres, community playing fields
Administration	Offices
Healthcare services	Hospitals, care homes
Construction and land-based industries	Construction sites, gardens, farms
Retail	Fashion stores, supermarkets
Public services	Fire stations, police stations, public transport

When you start work in sport or active leisure you may work any one of a number of different workplaces. You may work indoors at a sports centre or outdoor activity centre, a hospital or even a night club. Each environment will present different risks to your health and needs you to develop safe ways of working suitable for the situation.

Key term

Risk
The chances that an accident will happen.

Case study:

Outdoor water sports activity centre

If you work at an outdoor water sports activity centre you will be asked to work outdoors in all weathers – wind, sun, and rain. You will also be working in or on the water.

Activity: Water sports

Imagine you work in an outdoor water sports activity centre. What health and safety requirements would you have in the situations described in the case study? How would you prevent any health problems that might arise when you are at work?

Activity: Group discussion

If you work mainly indoors, you may not be in the sun or out in the wind, but you will have different health risks to worry about. What sort of health problems might be more likely in an indoor workplace? What could you do to prevent them?

Check

- There are many different work environments, or places of work

- Each one has different health risks and will need you to develop safe ways of working suitable to the situation.

L01 Health requirements

Health requirements at work are mostly shaped by the place where you work and the type of job that you do. If you consider the job you will be doing, and the place where you will work, you will have a good idea about what the health requirements for your job are.

For example, if you were working as a stable-hand at a stable you would need to:

- Wear protective clothing when working with horses
- Wash hands often to stop the spread of germs and disease
- Wear the right clothing for working both indoors and outdoors.

Here are some other examples:

Place of work	Health requirement	Why
Fitness club	Fitness and strength	To take exercise classes every day
Sports shop	Good posture	For being on your feet all day
Hospital	Good personal hygiene	To prevent spread of infection

Someone who works in a gym will sometimes need to lift heavy objects during the day, either to reposition gym equipment or give a demonstration, so will need to have good strength. A pool lifeguard must be able to concentrate for long periods of time to be sure that swimmers are safe.

Different jobs require different levels of personal fitness and different levels of concentration. Some jobs may be very active and exciting, while others can be quite boring. A lifeguard may be watching over only a few people in the pool who are simply swimming up and down slowly. In a hot and humid atmosphere, it can be difficult to concentrate.

Case study:

Different jobs, different health requirements

Faizal is a gym instructor, while Cathy is a ski instructor. Both work in different places and have different health requirements as a result.

Activity: Health checklist

Make a health checklist for both Faizal and Cathy, listing their health needs at work. Start by thinking about what a typical day means for them. Here are some questions to get you going:

- What personal health requirements do Cathy and Faizal's jobs require of them?
- Does working indoors have an impact?
- What about working outdoors in the snow?
- Are any special items of clothing required by either Cathy or Faizal? Why?

Activity: Your dream job

Think of your dream job in sport or active leisure. Think of what you would be doing and the activities you would be involved in. List the health requirements that the job would involve. Perhaps there is something you haven't thought of that would be a challenge for you? Make a poster to illustrate your thoughts and findings.

✓ Check

- Different places of work will present different health requirements
- The health requirements of a job may be shaped by the environment itself, the tasks involved, or the length or time of your shift
- Some jobs will need high levels of fitness or attention, requiring regular breaks to ensure freshness and good concentration.

L02 Health risks at work

Health requirements are also related to risks and hazards. You need to be able to identify the causes of risks and hazards to your health in your place of work.

A night club doorman may face verbal and physical abuse from drunken customers. A maintenance engineer in a swimming pool is at risk from chemicals used to treat swimming pool water.

Slip and trip hazards

Other risks include simple 'slip and trip' hazards caused by wet floors or stray cables left on a floor.

Lifting and transporting

Many jobs require you to lift or transport objects from one place to another. If you do not do this safely and correctly then you may seriously injure your back.

Stress

Some jobs, particularly those with greater responsibilities, can cause stress. Some stress is natural and generally good for us, but too much and not knowing how to cope with it will damage your health.

Hygiene

A café worker who fails to wash his or her hands properly, or fails to store food in the correct way, places not only employees' health at risk but also the health of customers as well.

Case study:

Café hygiene

Café manager fined for food safety offence – 30 April 2010

The manager of the Fast Track Caf , which leased premises from the Greater Bristol Active Leisure Centre, has been fined after his business was found to be in breach of food safety regulations. Trevor Brewster was ordered to pay £600 plus £2,450 costs when he appeared before Bristol Magistrates Court yesterday (Thursday). Environmental Health Officers visited Stevens' premises in November 2009 to carry out a routine inspection. They discovered raw meat was being stored in a dirty refrigeration unit alongside cooked meats, cheese and sandwich filling. Environmental Health Officer Brendan Delaney told the court that there had been a serious risk of cross-contamination which might have resulted in food poisoning. The Greater Bristol Active Leisure Centre made the decision earlier this year not to renew the lease to the Fast Track Caf . A new provider will be taking over from Fast Track in June.

Activity: Consequences

What were the health risks to the customers of this café? What were the consequences for its business?

Activity: Office work

Many jobs in sport and active leisure involve some office work. How many health risks can you see at this workstation?

✔ Check

- It is important you can spot the risks and hazards to your health in your place of work

- Look out for both major and minor health risks.

LO2 Reducing risks to your health

Equipment

When you are at work, it is important that you use the correct equipment in the correct way if you are to avoid illness or injury. For example, when you work at a computer, there are a number of factors that you need to consider to make sure that you do not strain or injure yourself. The components of your workstation need to be arranged in the right way. There are pieces of equipment, like keyboard shelves and document holders, that you can use to make sure you are comfortable.

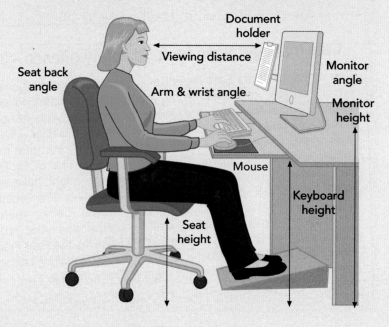

Components of a comfortable workstation

Activity: A comfortable workstation

Look at the list of factors below. What do you think are the health reasons for each one?

- Seat back angle
- Seat height
- Arm and wrist angle
- Keyboard height

- Monitor angle
- Viewing distance
- Document holder

Look back at the photo of the hazardous workstation over the page. How many health risks did you identify? Where there any that you missed?

Are there any changes you need to make to your workstation?

Many jobs are made easier and safer by using special equipment. For example, most outdoor public swimming pools have mechanical equipment for putting on and taking off pool covers. This job can be hazardous without this equipment. For jobs that involve lifting and transporting heavy objects, special equipment such as trolleys can help prevent injury.

Personal Protective Equipment

Personal Protective Equipment, or PPE, is another way of reducing risks. In sport, you wear shin pads, gloves or a helmet to prevent getting hurt playing sport. For some jobs at work, you may need to wear boots, goggles, gloves and overalls for the same reason.

Knowledge and training

Being more *aware* about the risks helps protect your health at work. Always read health and safety information leaflets or manuals provided by your employer and make sure you follow guidance about how to do jobs.

Activity: The right steps to reduce risk

Match the work activity to the health risk and method of reducing the risk.

Work activity	Health risk	Method of reducing risk
Outdoor activities instructor	High noise levels	Wear correct clothing
Swimming pool lifeguard	Illnesses, such as coughs and colds, etc.	Regular breaks
Fitness instructor	Abuse from fans	Use of PPE
Football manager	Exposure to electricity, gas, chemicals	Code of conduct for spectators
Sports centre engineer	Wind, rain, different temperatures	Annual vaccination

Check

- You must take steps to reduce the risks to your health in your place of work
- Always use special equipment for tasks when it is available
- Know the rules that apply to any jobs you carry out.

ASSESSMENT OVERVIEW

While working through this unit, you will have prepared for completing the following assessment tasks:

○	1.1	Explain different health requirements for a chosen area of work	Pages 38–41
○	2.1	Describe health risks for a chosen area of work	Pages 42–43
○	2.2	Explain how to reduce health risks in a chosen area of work	Pages 44–45

edexcel

Assignment tips

- Understand what is meant by the term *risk*

- Look at a number of sport and active leisure jobs to understand different health risks

- Visit a local sport and active leisure centre to see how centres reduce risks to people's health

- When at the centre, find out about what actions individual workers take to reduce risks to their health.

RISKS & HAZARDS IN SPORT & ACTIVE LEISURE

Anyone who takes part in sport and active leisure faces the risk of injury. Following a career in sport and active leisure will mean you need an understanding of health and safety in order to minimise the dangers. You also need to know how to act in emergency situations in the right way.

Every year there are thousands of sport- and active leisure-related injuries in the United Kingdom, both among professionals and among amateurs. Everyone who works in sport and active leisure needs to do everything they can to help reduce that number.

In this unit you will learn:

* How to keep people safe when they take part in sport and active leisure

* How to lower the risks to people when they take part in sport and active leisure

* How to act in the right way in a practice emergency situation

What happens if there is an accident?

L01 Keeping people safe

As the range of sport and active leisure activities available to people increases and more and more people want to take part, it is increasingly important that people working in this area can:

- Know about different types of risks and hazards

- Spot hazards and point them out to participants

- Take steps to reduce or get rid of these hazards.

Activity: Spot the hazards

In pairs, find as many possible hazards as you can. Which pieces of equipment do you think should be checked to make sure they are safe? Can you see any evidence that certain possible hazards have been thought about? Be ready to discuss with your class.

Functional skills

Talking about things with a partner will help you to develop your skills in **English**.

Questions to ask

- Is the weather a factor?

- Is the area where the activity is taking place suitable and clear of obstacles?

- Do participants have the right equipment and is it being used correctly?

- Are they wearing the right clothing and footwear for the activity?

- Is equipment not being used safely stored away and/or secured appropriately?

Activity: Accidents waiting to happen

Look at the following examples and say why an accident might happen:

1. A tiled floor in a swimming pool changing area has not been cleaned at the end of a previous session.

2. A trampoline has not been set up properly.

3. A netball court has not been checked for items such as glass, etc. before a match.

How would you respond? How would you make sure that these hazards are thought about next time?

Check

- Hazards are those things that can cause an accident or injury to people

- Risk refers to the chances that an accident will actually happen

- Protecting people from accidents in sport is very important.

L02 Reducing risks

Sport can never be completely safe. Accidents happen. But we must do as much as we can to *reduce* the number of hazards and the chances of an accident. Different sports have found different ways to achieve this.

In many sports, players wear clothing or equipment to protect them from injury.

Activity: Protection from injury

Can you think of a sport where equipment is worn to protect participants from injury? Make a list of items of protective clothing and equipment that participants wear for that sport.

Warning signs

Signs are another way of protecting people from possible hazards. Signs warn people about dangers. Your local swimming pool will have a number of signs displayed to guide swimmers on safety matters. These signs often use pictures to show the rules. For example, pools often have signs to say that running and jumping are not allowed.

Managing hazards at events

When people play or watch sport, people and facilities are put in place to control crowds, ensure that the rules are followed, and to provide first aid in the event of an accident. At football games, for example, stewards direct fans, police make sure that rival supporters are kept apart and ambulance services are provided. If a local club organises a tournament, they may ask the St John Ambulance to provide first aid.

Activity: Child's play

Extra care is taken with facilities used for children's play activities to protect them from the risk of serious injury. Can you identify the safety features of the way this play area has been designed and constructed?

- The play surface is made of a soft rubber-based material. How will this help?

- The trampoline is set at the same level as the floor. How does this help?

- The playground is surrounded by a tall wooden fence. Why is this?

✔ Check

- Risks and hazards must be reduced as much as possible

- Protective equipment, signs, specialist staff and well-designed sports and play areas all help to achieve this.

LO1 LO3 How to respond in an emergency

Accidents happen. In an **emergency**, you need to know what to do and how to respond.

In sport and active leisure, accidents may cause minor or major injuries.

Minor and major injuries

Minor injuries include strains, cuts and grazes. Major injuries include broken bones, head injuries, severe bleeding or unconsciousness. For a minor injury such as a cut or graze you should respond straightaway:

1. Assess the situation. Make sure that you are not at risk.

2. Reassure the casualty. Tell them your name, ask them what has happened and tell them what you are going to do.

3. Get help from a qualified person such as a first aider or similar.

When helping someone, make sure you follow health and safety guidance. For example, if a person has cut their leg and it is bleeding, do not touch the wound without putting on protective gloves.

If you are not qualified to deal with a situation, especially in the case of major injuries, find a person who is. Failure to do this could result in incorrect treatment or the injury being made worse.

In an emergency, communication is important. Giving clear instructions to a casualty will help the casualty relax. They know what you are doing and why.

Contacting emergency services

When contacting the emergency services, you need to be able to give full details of the emergency, where you are and how many casualties there are. Do you know the postcode for the venue you are at? An ambulance would need this to find you. Make sure that you give any information you are asked for clearly. Remain calm and follow any instructions given to you exactly.

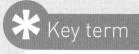

✱ Key term

Emergency
A serious, unexpected situation that needs to be dealt with immediately.

Written records

With any injury, it is important that a written record is made, and kept. There needs to be a record of what happened, who was involved, what injuries were sustained and the treatment that was given and by whom. The names and addresses of people injured, and of any witnesses, need to be recorded.

Activity: Group discussion

Why do you think it is important to keep these records?

Activity: Dealing with minor injuries

With a partner, choose a typical minor sports injury and find out how to deal with it. Role play how to deal with the injury to show the class.

Choose a major injury and repeat the activity.

Evacuations

A building or area may have to be evacuated in the event of fire, structural failure or natural disaster. How you react in these situations is very important if participants are not to be put in danger. Keep calm and follow instructions.

Functional skills

Writing a report when an injury happens will help you develop your skills in English.

Check

- Make sure you know how to respond to both minor and major injuries
- Make sure you have read and understood health and safety instructions
- In an emergency, take appropriate action *immediately,* get help if you are not qualified to deal with a situation and make sure you keep an accurate written record of what happened.

ASSESSMENT OVERVIEW

While working through this unit, you will have prepared for completing the following assessment tasks:

○	1.1	Identify potential hazards to people involved in sport and active leisure	Pages 48–49
○	1.2	Identify risks to people involved in sport and active leisure	Pages 48–49
○	2.1	Describe ways of minimising risks to people involved in sport and active leisure	Pages 50–51
○	3.1	Respond appropriately to a given, simulated emergency situation	Pages 52–53

edexcel :::

Assignment tips

- Practise trying to spot hazards in any areas used for sport and active leisure that you visit

- Know about typical risks faced by participants when taking part in a range of sports and active leisure activities, and how to reduce those risks

- Know how to deal with different kinds of emergency situations that occur in sport and active leisure. Practise your responses and ask your tutor to watch you to help you gather evidence to pass this unit.

- Know when and how to contact the emergency services and what information they will need from you.

TAKING PART IN EXERCISE & FITNESS

Exercise and fitness are big business today. People are more concerned about their health and fitness than ever before. There are many more gyms and health clubs now than there were even ten years ago to help people become fitter and healthier. These clubs offer a wide range of different ways of exercising, from group activities and classes to one to one time with a personal trainer. They need and are actively recruiting energetic, enthusiastic people with the right skills to deliver their services and help people exercise safely.

In this unit you will learn:

- About different ways of exercising and keeping fit, and different facilities that can be used

- How to exercise safely

- Work skills needed by someone working in exercise and fitness

- To look at your performance and say what went well and what could be improved

Why is it important to know about different exercise activities and facilities?

L01 Exercise & fitness activities

When we think of exercise and fitness activities, we tend to think of large, well-equipped fitness suites with young and healthy looking instructors supervising people taking an exercise class or perhaps lifting weights. But exercise and fitness involves a much wider range of activities than we might imagine.

Large fitness suites are fine for some people but not everybody can afford the time or the cost of using these facilities. Some people are put off exercising because they don't feel comfortable in a gym or with modern day fitness equipment. Other people are not motivated to exercise at all and need encouragement to find a suitable activity and participate.

Exercise and fitness activities take place indoors and outdoors and include activities designed specifically for exercise, such as aerobics or boxercise, as well as more traditional competitive sports. People exercise on their own or in groups or classes.

Activity: Outdoor activities

With a partner, make a list of outdoor activities that are regarded as 'exercise and fitness' activities. How many different activities can you think of?

With both indoor and outdoor activities, a variety of factors such as age, income, availability of facilities and the time a person has available all influence the type of activity a person chooses to take part in.

Equipment

For people choosing to exercise in a cardio-vascular gym, a range of equipment is usually available. This may include rowing machines, exercise bikes and treadmills which make the heart pump more blood around the body, as well as resistance machines and free weights for building upper body strength.

✳ Key term

Cardio-vascular
This refers to the heart (cardio) and blood vessels (vascular).

Activity: Gym equipment

With a partner visit a local gym or fitness club. Make a list of the different items of equipment available and what each is for. Draw diagrams or take photographs and write a description of what you do when you exercise using each piece of equipment.

Activity: Group discussion

Many people use a gym to train for another sport. For each of the items of equipment you listed and described in the previous activity, try to give at least two examples of sports that each exercise would be good for.

✔ Check

- There are many different ways to exercise

- You can exercise individually or in classes or groups

- A range of equipment is available to help people get fitter, including exercise bikes, treadmills, rowing machines and weights.

L01 Exercise & fitness facilities

There are three main types of **facilities**. Facilities are usually either *public* or *private* or they may be run by a *voluntary* association or club. These different types of facility are sometimes referred to as *sectors*. They describe how a facility is managed and run.

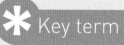

✳ Key term

Facilities
Buildings or equipment provided for exercise and fitness.

Public sector

Public sector facilities are run by the local council or authority. They include school and college facilities, as well as local sports halls, swimming pools, leisure centres, and even sometimes village halls.

These facilities are provided for local people at a price they can afford. Often this means that the facilities are fairly basic. They may not be as high quality as those in the private sector. Local councils are more concerned with providing services than they are with making money.

Private sector

Private sector facilities, like the one shown below, are run by businesses. Their facilities are often of higher quality than those provided in the public

sector because they can charge as much as they need to make a profit. State of the art facilities are provided by David Lloyd and Bannatyne's centres. Bannatyne's is the largest independent operator of health clubs, with over 60 facilities. Other providers include Livingwell, LA Fitness, Cannons, and Esporta.

This sector also includes individual trainers and fitness instructors who visit your home or run classes of their own in local facilities which they rent. In many communities, a wide range of fitness activities is offered by individual providers.

Voluntary sector

The voluntary sector includes all kinds of clubs and activities which are organised by participants themselves for themselves. So a group of friends might meet regularly to go jogging together, or they might use a local park or green space to gather for exercise. Voluntary activities also include people who exercise on their own at home using exercise videos, for example, or Wii Fit.

Activity: Mapping local facilities

Make a copy of a map of your local area. With a partner, pool your knowledge of the local area and mark all the places on the map where people exercise. Colour code your marks, with public facilities in blue, private facilities in red, and parks and other spaces where people exercise together or individually in green. Make a list for each type of facility.

Check

- Facilities are managed and run in different ways
- They may be owned and managed by public, private or voluntary sector providers.

L02 Gathering information

People who want to take part in an exercise activity need access to information about what is available.

Providing information

Customers need to know:

- What is available
- When facilities are open and what activities are available
- How much different activities cost.

A facility that does not provide the public with enough information will have very few customers. The more ways a centre can provide information, the more customers they are likely to attract.

Information sources

Ways of sharing information with potential customers include telephone directories, local newspapers, posters or leaflets in doctors' surgeries, radio adverts, the internet, posters on community noticeboards and by taking a stand at local events to talk to people about what is available.

Word of mouth

Perhaps the most important way information is shared is by 'word of mouth'. This is where a customer tells friends and others about an activity or centre they have enjoyed. Think of how important it is to your decisions, when a close friend recommends a film, a club or a restaurant. It is much more likely you will go yourself if you hear about it from someone you know.

Functional skills

Reading information sources will help you develop your skills in **English**.

Activity: Sharing information about activities and facilities

Choose two local fitness facilities and find out the different ways they use to provide information for potential customers. Ask if you can have a few minutes to talk to the centre manager about how they do this. Gather any information leaflets or brochures that they may provide which will tell you about the fitness activities they offer. Visit each centre's website to see what information they provide there.

Now imagine you are an elderly person, a young mum and a working man. Do the centres provide information for these potential customers? How? Do you think that the way they have chosen to share information about services to each of these different people works? What would you do differently to do the job better?

Check

- Sharing information with possible customers is important for your business or activity to succeed

- People find out about how and where to exercise from a range of sources

- Some of these sources of information are better than others for reaching different groups of people.

L02 Safe exercise & fitness

Warm up and cool down

You should always warm up before exercising and cool down after exercising. This helps to stop you getting injured and reduces how sore you feel after the activity. Look at the diagrams below to see what a warm up and cool down should include.

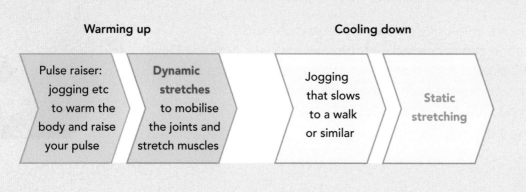

Warming up

Pulse raiser: jogging etc to warm the body and raise your pulse → **Dynamic stretches** to mobilise the joints and stretch muscles

Cooling down

Jogging that slows to a walk or similar → **Static stretching**

◎ Activity: Go for a run

Go out for a run with a friend. Share the exercise that you do to warm up before you start your run and cool down at the end.

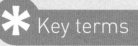

✳ Key terms

Static stretches
Stretches done standing still.

Dynamic stretches
Stretches that involve slow, steady movement.

Functional skills

Explaining how to do a warm up could help you improve skills in English.

Staff assistance

When you are engaged in any type of exercise or fitness activity, the advice and assistance of qualified staff is an important resource.

There are two different types of staff in fitness facilities: *dry side* and *wet side* staff. Wet side staff work in swimming and leisure pools, while dry side staff work in sports halls and fitness areas. For example, lifeguards are on hand to supervise people using the pool and deal with any incidents that may happen. Leisure attendants are trained to set up equipment correctly and look out for any possible accidents. Sports coaches will teach you the correct techniques for the sport you are playing. All facilities will have someone on site who is trained in first aid.

Induction

The advice and assistance of staff is especially important if you are new to exercise. You need to know how to exercise and use equipment safely so that you do not injure or harm yourself. When you are getting started with a new activity you will need help to make sure that you understand what to do and what you should avoid. This is called an induction. An induction will take you through a number of steps. These include:

- A screening exercise to make sure you are healthy enough to exercise

- A demonstration to show you how to use equipment safely

- Questions about what you want to achieve so that your instructor can help you design a suitable fitness programme

- A demonstration and/or questions to make sure you know how to warm up and cool down correctly at the start and end of each fitness session.

Key term

Induction
Instruction for beginners in how to exercise and use equipment safely.

Activity: Practice induction

Choose a piece of equipment you know how to use for exercise. Take a partner through an induction on how to use this equipment. Ask your tutor to observe you doing this and give feedback.

 Functional skills

Doing an induction will help you practise your speaking and listening skills for English.

✓ Check

- You should warm up and cool down before and after exercise

- All facilities have staff who are there to help you exercise safely

- All people new to exercise or to a particular activity should receive an *induction* in how to exercise and use equipment safely.

L03 Workplace qualities

Many of the qualities that you need when taking part in exercise and fitness activities will also be required at work. You need to take an *active* part in what you are doing. This means:

- Showing enthusiasm
- Being motivated
- Being willing to have a go
- Having positive body language
- Taking a positive attitude.

Enthusiasm

You need to put energy into what you do. Sometimes this requires effort. If you are positive and enthusiastic about what you are doing, you will enjoy it too.

Motivation

People who are motivated keep the reasons why they are taking part clearly in focus at all times. If you have no reason to exercise, you will be more likely to give up on what you are doing. It is much harder to exercise without any clear goals in mind.

People exercise for many different reasons. They may exercise to:

- Lose weight, tone up or relieve stress
- Prepare for a specific event, like a triathlon
- Recover from an illness, such as a heart problem.

Some people exercise simply because they enjoy it.

Being willing to have a go

There is a wide range of exercise activities available. It is important to be open minded and willing to try a range of activities to find out which is right for you. If you are unwilling to try new activities, you may settle for an activity that is not right for you.

Body language

When you take part in exercise, you body language says a great deal about what you think and feel and your readiness to participate. In a tennis session, if you are on your toes and you are gripping the racket well, you will be much more likely to react in the right way when your coach feeds you the ball.

Activity: Positive body language

Positive body language is also important at work. Look closely at these photos. Which of the two has positive body language? Why? Think about the difference in their facial features, the way they are holding their hands and the way they are dressed.

Activity: Mood board

Make a mood board showing what you are enthusiastic about and what is motivating you currently, and what you feel negative about and is wasting your energy. See if you can identify areas where you need to rethink your approach and show a more positive attitude. This should help you express new goals in relation to sport and exercise.

✔ Check

- You need to take an *active* part in what you are doing

- Have a *goal* to aim for will help you

- Be willing to try a range of activities to find the right one for you.

L03 Workplace skills

Time management

When you are given a task, do you usually complete it in the time available? If not, why not? Is it because you waste time or do you put things off until another time?

In exercise activities, good time-keeping means arriving on time for a class or exercise session and being ready to start as soon as you arrive. At work, your employer will expect the same. If you are unable to manage your time well, then you will find it very difficult to be an effective employee for an organisation. Any job that you do will require you to carry out certain tasks at a set time each day or week for example.

Being serious about taking exercise will teach you the same skills you will need if you are going to be serious about your career.

Dressing appropriately

If you are taking exercise regularly, you are required to adopt the right dress code. In other words, you need to dress appropriately for the activity. For most exercise activities it is important that your clothes fit well and allow you to move freely. If you look the part, it will help you have a positive attitude and communicate to others that you are serious about what you are doing. Wearing the right clothing also helps prevent accidents and injuries.

Activity: Dressed for fitness

Look at this image. How are the fitness instructor and the client dressed? What does this say about them and their attitude? How will the way they are dressed affect the way they work together?

Health and safety

It is important to think about both your own and others' health and safety.

There are a number of laws which give employers, employees and clients important responsibilities when it comes to health and safety.

An instructor should make you aware of a number of health and safety issues during an induction before starting any new exercise.

1. The instructor shows the client, and explains in detail, how to use each piece of equipment required for an activity.

2. The instructor makes sure that the client warms up and cools down properly.

3. The instructor makes sure that the client is wearing appropriate clothing.

Activity: Group discussion

Why is an induction necessary? What might happen if a person new to an activity did not receive this attention?

Activity: Self-assessment

For a period of time that you can agree with your tutor, keep a diary or notebook about the exercise and fitness activities you currently take part in. Make a record of the date and time of each session, where the activity took place, and how you felt you performed. Describe what you wore for each activity and why, how you showed good time management and how you showed the ability to follow instructions. Show how you thought about and acted to protect your own and others' health and safety.

Check

- Your timekeeping and appearance are very important

- Think carefully about health and safety and always follow instructions.

L04 Reviewing your performance

Both in exercise and in work, it is important that you are able to review your performance to find out what can be improved or developed further. By doing this, you will know *what* to improve and this will then help you to decide *how* to improve.

We can review our performance as follows:

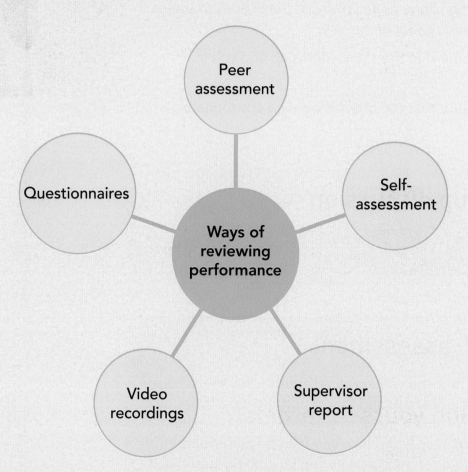

See Unit 6 for information about the different ways of reviewing performance.

Goals

To improve your performance, you must set yourself a goal – a target you want to reach. This could be a *short* or a *long-term* goal. Once you have set yourself a target, you can then decide on how to help yourself achieve this target. You may need a group or class to help motivate you. Perhaps you may need to buy yourself some new sports clothing?

Case study:

Laura Woodman

Laura has recently had her yearly appraisal with her gym instructor, Lewis. They discussed how Laura had performed over the last year, what had gone well and what might be improved in the programme she had been following. Laura was happy that she had lost the weight she had hoped for, but found some of the sessions boring. Lewis felt that Laura could push herself harder at times and was also concerned that Laura often seemed to be late for classes.

Activity: Steps towards the goal

What could Laura do to improve her performance? Suggest three things she could do to help herself towards the goal of improving her fitness levels over the next 12 months. How would setting a goal help this?

Activity: Setting yourself targets

Choose an exercise activity that you are currently involved in. Suggest three ways you could help yourself to improve.

✓ Check

- To improve your exercise and fitness performance, you need goals to aim for

- There are ways that you can help yourself towards achieving your goals.

ASSESSMENT OVERVIEW

While working through this unit, you will have prepared for completing the following assessment tasks:

○	1.1	Describe different exercise and fitness activities	Page 56
○	1.2	Identify different exercise and fitness facilities	Page 58–59
○	2.1	Describe an induction process for an exercise and fitness activity	Page 63
○	2.2	Describe warm-up and cool-down activities	Page 62
○	3.1	Actively participate in exercise and fitness activities and demonstrate: • time management skills • appropriate dress for the activity • following instructions provided by the activity leader • following health and safety guidelines before, during and after activities	Pages 64–67
○	4.1	Identify your strengths and areas for improvement in exercise and fitness activities	Pages 68–69
○	4.2	Suggest ways of improving your performance in one activity	Pages 68–69

edexcel

Assignment tips

- Gather information about local facilities and about as many different ways of exercising as you can. Work with a partner and share what you find out.

- Speak to a fitness instructor at a local centre about what they do to warm up and cool down clients

- Keep a diary or notebook about your taking part in different exercises and ask for feedback from tutors or friends about how you are doing. Keep a record of any comments they make.

- Sit down and think about what you could do better. Be as honest with yourself as you can.

HOW THE BODY WORKS

If you take part in sport or exercise your body needs to be able to react immediately to supply muscles with energy for what you are trying to do. It is important to know how your body achieves this so that you can prepare in the right way for sport and exercise.

In this unit you will learn:

- What the skeleton and muscles are for
- How the heart and lungs work
- What makes up a healthy diet

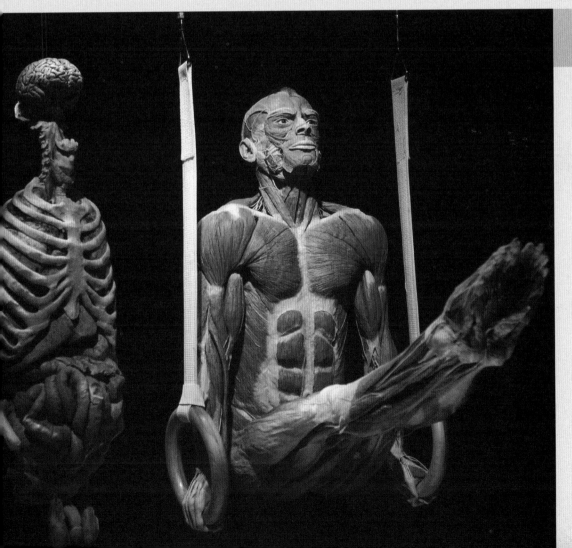

How does the body work when it's working right?

L01 The skeleton

The skeleton supplies the body's framework, to which other parts of the body are attached. It protects the important organs and provides the body's structure. The skeleton consists of two main parts:

- The axial skeleton is the main part of the skeleton, on which everything else 'hangs'.

- The appendicular skeleton includes all the other bones that attach to the central axial skeleton. This includes your arms and legs.

Did you know?

- When you are born, you have 300 bones in your body, but by the time you are an adult you have only 206

- Bones are 50 per cent water

- The strongest bone in your body is your femur (your thigh bone)

- There are 14 bones in your face, 8 in each wrist and 23 in each foot.

Activity: Amazing bones

Think about each of the facts given above and study the picture of the skeleton opposite. Can you think of reasons why the bones are shaped the way they are?

Joints

This is how all movement in your body takes place. Muscles work in pairs to move bones at places called *joints*.

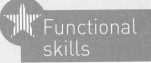

Functional skills

Explaining what muscles are for will help you develop your skills in **English**.

Activity: Find your muscles

With a partner, and using the diagram on this page, locate the major muscles on your bodies. Make sticky labels of each of these muscles. Stick your labels over the areas of your partners body where these muscles are located.

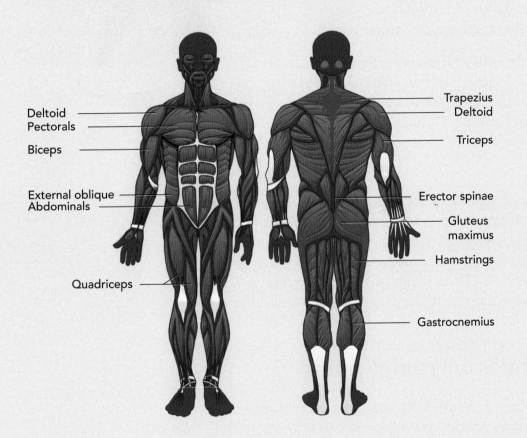

Deltoid
Pectorals
Biceps
External oblique
Abdominals
Quadriceps

Trapezius
Deltoid
Triceps
Erector spinae
Gluteus maximus
Hamstrings
Gastrocnemius

✔ Check

- Some muscles work on their own, other muscles can be controlled
- The heart muscle works on its own to pump blood around the body
- Muscles either contract (get shorter) or relax (get longer) and they pull on bones to cause movement.

L02 The cardio-respiratory system

The cardio-respiratory system is made up of the heart and the lungs. 'Cardio' refers to the heart. 'Respiratory' refers to the breathing of the lungs.

The heart

The heart is a muscular pump with four chambers.

1. It pumps blood from the heart to the lungs and back again to get fresh oxygen.

2. Then it pumps this blood from the heart everywhere else to move the oxygen around the body and pick up waste products that the body no longer needs.

Your heart is two pumps in one. The right side sends deoxygenated blood (blood without any oxygen left in it) to the lungs to become oxygenated, while the left side sends this oxygenated blood around the body.

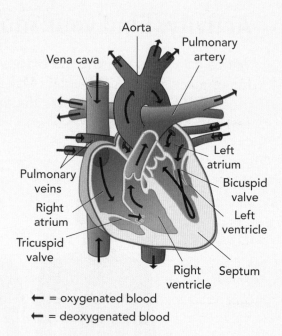

← = oxygenated blood
← = deoxygenated blood

The heart beat

In a typical day, your heart will beat over 87,000 times. When you play sport or take part in a physical activity, your heart rate (the number of times your heart beats per minute), speeds up to pump more blood around the body and get more oxygen to the working muscles. When you are at rest, your heart pumps about five litres of blood around the body every minute. When you exercise very hard this can rise to 20, or even as much as 40 litres.

Activity: Find your radial pulse

Working with a partner, sit relaxed in a chair while your partner takes your pulse. Your partner should count the number of beats in 30 seconds and then double this number. This is your resting pulse rate. Now lie on the floor and have your partner repeat this. Finally, stand up and have your partner repeat this once more. What differences did you find? Can you think of a reason for these differences?

The heart's other important functions

The heart makes sure that nutrients in the blood are spread to the whole body. It also spreads heat from the centre of your body to the skin on the outside so that your body keeps at the right temperature.

Activity: Knowing your heart

Ask your tutor for an unlabelled diagram of the heart for you to label. Show the route the blood takes through the heart. Include notes on the different functions of the heart.

The respiratory system

The respiratory system works with the heart to deliver oxygen to the body and remove carbon dioxide. Air enters the nose and mouth and goes down to the lungs through a large tube called the *trachea*. At the lungs, it splits into two *bronchi*. These now spread like a tree in the lungs getter smaller and thinner and becoming *bronchioles* and ending in tiny sacs called *alveoli*. This is where oxygen and carbon dioxide are exchanged.

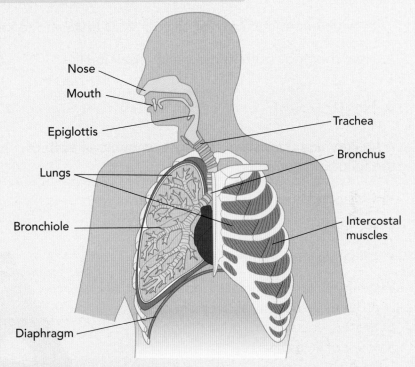

Nose
Mouth
Epiglottis
Lungs
Bronchiole
Diaphragm
Trachea
Bronchus
Intercostal muscles

Activity: Knowing how we breathe

Ask your tutor for an unlabelled diagram of the respiratory system for you to label. Include notes about the functions of the respiratory system. Show the passage of air into the lungs and the direction of the flow of oxygen and carbon dioxide.

✓ Check

- The respiratory system gets oxygen into the body and carbon dioxide out
- The heart circulates blood around the body, carrying oxygen and nutrients that the body needs
- Unlike other muscles that rest when they are not being used, the heart never stops beating.

L03 A healthy diet

Nutrition

Everything the body does requires energy. The body's energy comes from the **nutrients** in the food you eat. Your diet has to:

1. Provide enough energy for all your daily tasks and to keep you warm.

2. Help the body both to grow and repair itself.

A healthy diet

A healthy diet consists of the right amounts of each of the following nutrients:

- Carbohydrates
- Proteins
- Minerals and vitamins
- Fats
- Water

Water is contained in most foods you eat, but in order to be healthy and remain properly **hydrated**, you need to drink the right amount of fluids also.

Carbohydrates provide most of the energy you need. They include pasta, potatoes and rice. Protein comes from meat, fish, eggs and dairy produce. Fruit and vegetables provide vitamins and minerals. The fat you need comes from meat, cheese, nuts, and cooking oils. The diagram shows how much food from each group you need each day.

Use sparingly – fats, oils, sweets

2 portions of meat, fish, eggs, beans and peas

3 portions of milk cheese and yoghurt

4 portions of fruit and vegetables

6 portions of bread and vegetables

FORTIFIED BREAKFAST CEREAL

Rich in vitamin B's

250g

> **Key term**
>
> **Nutrition (nutrients)**
> What the body needs to stay healthy.
>
> **Hydration (hydrated)**
> How much water there is in the body.

Activity: Planning for what you eat

Think about how much you eat in a day. Compare your normal diet with how much extra you eat on days when you are exercising. Now try to come up with a basic menu for three days, spreading your intake over three main meals, but adding snacks in to suit your needs and schedule. Two of those days should include enough extra food to give you energy for exercise.

Hydration

As well as eating enough of the right food each day, you also need to drink enough water to keep your body hydrated. Your body is using up water all the time, through breathing, urination and sweating. When you are taking part in sport or active leisure you use the water up more quickly than usual.

How much should I drink?

As a rough guide, you should drink *half* of your body weight (measured in pounds) in ounces of water a day. The Food Standards Agency advises you to drink six to eight glasses of water a day. If you take part in sport or active leisure, you will need to drink even more.

About 20% of the water you need comes from the food you eat. This means that you need to *drink* the other 80%. Drink little and often. Drinking too much water can be almost as bad as not drinking enough. If your urine is a light colour and is produced in good amounts then your hydration is about right.

Activity: Think drink!

Make a poster that reminds members of a gym of how important it is to drink. Include guidance about when and how much to drink.

Check

- The body's strength comes from the nutrients and energy it gets from the food you eat
- A healthy diet consists of carbohydrates, protein, fat, vitamins and minerals
- Drinking enough fluid is also important.

ASSESSMENT OVERVIEW

While working through this unit, you will have prepared for completing the following assessment tasks:

○	1.1	Identify the functions of the skeleton	Pages 74–75
○	1.2	Identify the functions of the muscular system	Pages 76–77
○	2.1	Identify the structure and function of the heart	Pages 78–79
○	2.2	Identify the structure and function of the lungs	Pages 79
○	3.1	Identify the different nutrients needed for a healthy diet	Pages 80–81
○	3.2	Identify the functions of each nutrient	Pages 80–81

Assignment tips

- Make sure you know where each of the major bones are in the body

- Make sure you know where each of the major muscles are in the body

- Look at what you eat and drink each day and tell yourself why you need each item

- Keep a notebook to record the amount of fluid you drink each day to see if you are drinking enough

- Try to explain to a friend what the cardio-respiratory system is made up of, how it works, and the function of each part.

PLANNING OWN FITNESS PROGRAMME

This unit looks at the different parts of fitness and the training that is available for each part. It follows on from *Unit 11 Taking part in exercise and fitness*.

To play sport well, you need a certain level of fitness. One way to improve your performance is to improve your fitness levels. In this unit, you will again have the chance to participate actively in training activities. You will also cover basic fitness testing, which will help you decide if the training you are doing is meeting the goals you set for it and what you need to do to improve.

In this unit you will learn:

- About the different parts of physical fitness
- How to find out how fit you are
- How to get fitter using a fitness plan
- How to get over barriers to getting fitter
- To look at your own fitness plan and say what went well and what could be improved

Why might a sportsperson like Chris Hoy need to plan their own fitness programme?

L01 What is physical fitness?

When taking part in sport or active leisure, certain physical fitness components are needed to do it successfully. The higher your sporting involvement, the higher the fitness levels you will need.

Case study:
Lionel Messi

Lionel Messi plays for Barcelona football club and is described as perhaps the world's best player. He is an attacking forward who is there to score goals. A football game lasts 90 minutes and in that game he may cover 6–7 miles by running, jogging, sprinting and walking. He has to beat defenders to get free to shoot at goal and needs to be able to hold off an opponent who is trying to take the ball from him.

Activity: Messi's fitness components

List the different fitness components that you think Messi needs to be one of the best players in the world. Give an example of how each fitness component helps make him a great football player.

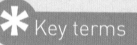
Key terms

Component
Part of something much larger. A fitness component is one part of your total fitness.

Fitness components

There are five main fitness components. They are:

- Aerobic endurance (or stamina)
- Flexibility
- Strength
- Speed
- Body composition.

Aerobic endurance/stamina

The heart and lungs supply oxygen to the working muscles in the body. This means we can keep an activity going for a long time. A marathon runner is very good at doing this.

Flexibility

This is the range of movement at a joint. It lets us do a wide range of movements, from a tennis serve to a somersault in gymnastics. It also means we avoid injuries when playing.

Strength

Strength is how much 'pull' a muscle or group of muscles can make in one effort. Weightlifters need to have very high levels of strength to raise weights above their head.

Speed

This is quickness of movement. In 2009 Usain Bolt ran the 100 metres in 9.58 seconds – an average speed of almost 24 miles per hour!

Body composition

This is the make-up of the body in terms of muscle and fat. There are three main body types, shown in the diagram on the right.

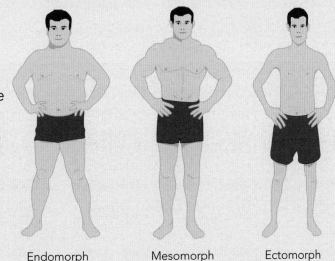

Endomorph   Mesomorph   Ectomorph

Activity: What's best for you?

Think of a sport that you play. List the different fitness components you need and give a reason why each one is needed. Which body shape is best suited to your sport? Why?

Check

- All sports and active leisure activities need fitness
- Different sports require different levels of each component depending on what the sport or activity requires the performer to do.

L01 How fit are you?

Before making your own fitness plan or programme, you must know what your current fitness levels are. To do this you can measure your fitness using a range of fitness tests. There are over 100 recognised tests for fitness.

Activity: The Cooper 12-minute run

This test is used to measure aerobic endurance (stamina). In this test, travel as far as you can around a 400-metre track in 12 minutes. First warm up, then run or walk as far as possible in 12 minutes. Record the distance travelled to the nearest 100 m and then cool down. Compare your distance using the table below (← means 'less than' and → means 'more than').

Age	Poor	Below average	Average	Above average	Excellent
Males 13–14	←2100 m	2100–2199 m	2200–2399 m	2400–2700 m	→2700 m
Females 13–14	←1500 m	1500–1599 m	1600–1899 m	1900–2000 m	→2000 m
Males 15–16	←2200 m	2200–2299 m	2300–2499 m	2500–2800 m	→2800 m
Females 15–16	←1600 m	1600–1699 m	1700–1999 m	2000–2100 m	→2100 m
Males 17–19	←2300 m	2300–2499 m	2500–2699 m	2700–3000 m	→3000 m
Females 17–19	←1700 m	1700–1799 m	1800–2099 m	2100–2300 m	→2300 m

There are tests for other areas of your fitness as well.

Strength

Strength can be measured using a hand grip dynamometer (pictured). This measures grip strength.

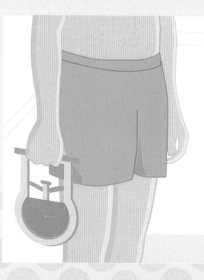

Flexibility

This is how much movement is possible at a joint. A simple way to measure how flexible you are is to use the 'sit and reach' test.

Activity: The 'sit and reach' test

Look at the photo for an illustration of how to do this test. Do not wear shoes and place your feet flat against the box. Notice the 15 cm 'overhang' of the box. Keeping your legs unbent, slowly reach forwards as far as you can while a helper reads how far your fingertips reach along the scale. For a male under the age of 35, a score of 45 cm or more is excellent. For a woman, the excellent score starts at 46 cm.

! Remember

Warm up properly and have practice tests before taking a score.

Speed

Speed can be measured by a number of tests. One example is the timed 35 metre sprint test.

Body composition

Use the hip-to-waist ratio test. In this test, measure (in centimetres) your waist at your belly button and your hips at their widest point. Divide your waist measurement by your hip measurement to calculate your score.

Functional skills

Working out your score for different fitness tests will help you develop your skills in **mathematics**.

Activity: Hip-to-waist ratio test

Carry out a hip-to-waist ratio test on yourself. Then find a hip-to-waist ratio results table to check your own hip-to-waist ratio score. Your tutor should be able to help you find one.

✓ Check

- Fitness tests help you work out how fit you are
- There are different kinds of test for different areas of fitness.

L02
L03
Using a fitness programme

A **fitness programme**, or fitness plan, will help you get fitter. It sets out what **training activities** will be done and when. Before you plan your own fitness programme, it is important that you decide on a number of things.

✳ Key terms

Fitness programme
A plan of activities to improve someone's fitness.

Training activities
The actions that are put into a fitness programme.

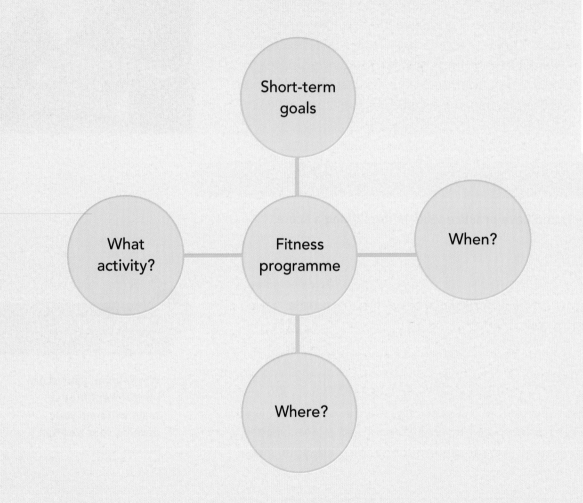

- *Short-term goals*: What is it you want to achieve from the programme? Weight loss? Bigger biceps? Increased muscle tone? Losing a few inches from your bottom or tummy?

- *When?*: What time of the day can you train? At what time are the classes that you want to take part in available?

- *Where?*: Where are the classes/facilities that you will need to use?

- *What activity?*: What activity do you want to do? Running? Swimming? Working out in a gym?

These questions will really affect your plan. Make sure you think about them carefully.

Case study:
Ice hockey goalkeeper

Steve is an ice hockey goalkeeper who has been playing for some time and finds himself in a rut. He has reached a level of success based mainly on his natural talent but wants to be a better player and achieve more success.

Steve is not sure how to move forward. He knows he needs to be fitter on the ice, but is not sure how to achieve this. His ice hockey skills are good, but he finds that his performance in the final period of the game gets worse and worse.

He has good local facilities (including the rink where he plays), local gyms and a sports hall, plus a range of parks and countryside where outdoor facilities are available. But how should he move forward and what should he do?

Activity: Write a fitness programme

Write a short report about why you want to train. Identify a short-term goal you want to achieve. Describe the training activities you enjoy and plan a short training period using different training methods. Measure your fitness levels before and after the training programme to see what effects there have been on your fitness. Decide when and where you are going to train and produce a written plan to show this.

Functional skills

Writing a fitness plan for yourself will help develop your skills in English.

Activity: Daily improvement

Think of one thing you could do every day to improve your fitness.

Check

- Make sure you think everything through carefully before making your plan
- The more suited your plan is to you, the more likely you are to stick to it.

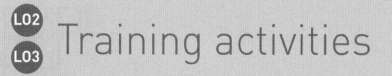

LO2 LO3 Training activities

You can train indoors or outdoors, at home or in a special facility. Your main decision will be what type of training activity you do and when. This depends on *why* you are training.

Different training activities

Type of activity	What you will do	Benefit	Examples
Interval training	This is where you work for a set period of time followed by a set rest period	Trains the heart to recover quickly, which is useful in sports	• Circuit training • Interval running
Resistance training	This is where you train against some kind of force working against you	Improves your strength in various parts of the body	• Resistance machines in the gym • Free weights
Flexibility training	This is where you stretch different muscles and tendons in your body	Increases movement at your joints and helps reduce the chances of injury	• Static stretching (one example is pictured) • Passive stretching • Active stretching
Speed training	This is where you move your body at speed	Makes your movement quicker and more effective	• Acceleration training • Sprint drills

Case study:

Gymnastic training

Sarah is a gymnast. She is currently training to compete in the Olympics. Her fitness programme has been developed to include activities that work together and build different aspects of her fitness so that she can perform to the best of her ability at the games.

Sarah's programme is not just about working on gymnastics equipment, although this is a big part of her training programme. She also does strength training to develop the muscles and strength she needs to perform her routines. To make sure this happens, her fitness programme begins with two hours of strength training in the gym every day.

Activity: Complementary training

Think about your current fitness programme. Is there anything you could add to it that would fit in with what you are already doing?

Check

- Choose activities you enjoy and are able to do
- Think about how the activities you do fit together.

L04 Barriers to getting fit

So far you have put together a well-designed fitness programme. Now it's important to think about what might get in the way of you achieving the goals included in that programme.

There are many factors that can have an effect on what you achieve. These factors are called barriers.

Time

Time is the major factor that affects the goals you set. The amount of time you are able to give to your training will affect how much you improve. Factors include:

- Study patterns and any other regular commitments (such as part-time work)

- Family commitments (such as looking after relatives or going on a family holiday)

- The time that the facilities are available to use.

Overcoming this barrier can be achieved by setting aside specific times to train. You may be able to exercise at school, at college or at work. For example, some employers provide their staff with access to gym facilities.

And simple changes to your day might help you be more active. For instance, walking or cycling instead of catching the bus can be a useful change.

Here are the main barriers and possible solutions to them:

Barrier	Explanation	Problem it causes	Possible solution
Time	Your study/work and family commitments will affect how much time you have to train	Lack of time will affect how many times you can train and for how long	• Train before going home • Train at work or college/school during your lunch break • Train while travelling
Cost	How much spare money you have will affect how many times you can train	May affect how many times you train each week or the range of facilities you use	• Look for money-saving offers • Try to make savings in other areas • Try to think of 'real world' alternatives to using a gym
Location	The range of facilities that are available for you to use	Living in the countryside might mean there are fewer places to train	• Be flexible and try different training activities
Motivation	How much you want to train	Lack of motivation will affect the effort you make and how often you get out and train	• Train with a friend or in a group • Have targets to achieve • Measure improvements

> **✳ Key terms**
>
> **Goals**
> Targets to aim for. They can be short-term, medium-term or long-term.
>
> **Barriers**
> Things that may prevent you from achieving the goals included in your fitness programme.

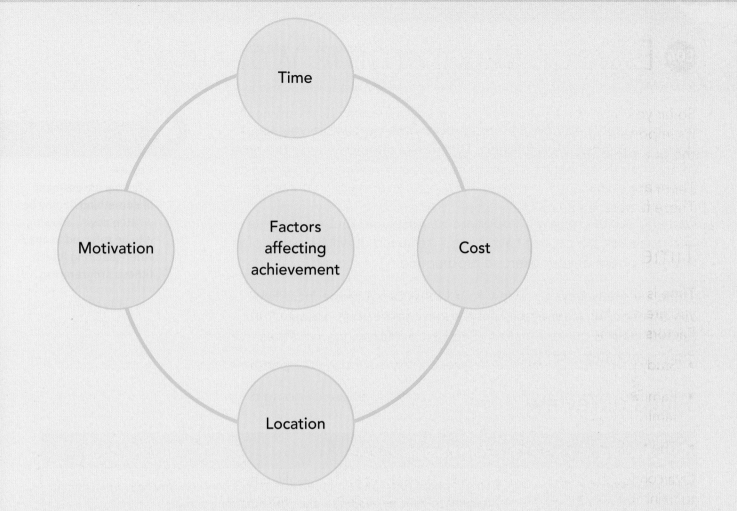

Activity: Assessing your barriers

Talk to a friend about the barriers that could affect your training. How could you overcome these barriers? Give some examples to your partner. Try to find examples of others who have faced similar barriers as you and how they have overcome them.

Check

- Look for barriers to your training and decide how they can be tackled

- Have a goal or target that you want to achieve.

L05 Is your programme working?

It is important to **review** a fitness programme both while you are doing it and after it has finished. This review should include the type of activity carried out, the level of motivation present and the facility being used.

Carrying out the review is important to make sure that any targets and goals set can be – or have been – achieved. It will help you plan the next phase of your exercise programme.

There are many ways to review your fitness programme including self-assessment, peer assessment, supervisor reports, video recordings and questionnaires. (See *Unit 6 Improving own fitness* for more information about these.)

Types of review

Type of review	What happens
Self-assessment	This is where you look at yourself and assess how well you have been doing. It might be done by keeping a diary or something similar
Peer assessment	A friend or colleague gives feedback or a written observation on how well you have been doing
Supervisor report	Same as above but more formal
Video recordings	Practical activities are recorded on video-recording equipment, allowing comparisons to be made with previous attempts at the same activity
Questionnaires	Forms with questions designed to find out how you are doing

Reviewing your fitness programme is really important. It will tell you if you have achieved the goals you set yourself at the start. You will need to decide on a way of reviewing your training programme that works for you.

For example, you could weigh yourself at the end of the programme to see how much weight you have lost, or repeat fitness tests to see how much you have improved a fitness component. Your review might simply be that you successfully complete an event you were training for.

Activity: Presenting your progress

Design a short presentation to give on how your own fitness programme is going.

Functional skills

Explaining your progress to others will help you to develop your skills in **English**.

Check

- A review will tell you what went well and what needs to be changed

- There are a number of ways of reviewing your programme

- Choose the way of doing a review that suits you best.

ASSESSMENT OVERVIEW

While working through this unit, you will have prepared for completing the following assessment tasks:

○	1.1	Describe the components of physical fitness	Pages 84–85
○	2.1	Assess your own fitness levels	Pages 86–87
○	3.1	With guidance, plan your own fitness programme with set targets	Pages 88–91
○	3.2	Use your own fitness programme over a given period of time	Pages 88–91
○	4.1	Identify barriers to achieving fitness goals	Pages 92–93
○	4.2	Identify ways to overcome barriers	Pages 92–93
○	5.1	Assess the results of your own fitness programme	Pages 94–95

edexcel

Assignment tips

- Look at a range of different activities and identify what fitness components they need and why

- Have targets and goals for your training programme

- Choose activities you enjoy and that use local facilities

- Use a range of ways to assess your programme. Keep a diary as well.

ASSISTING A LEADER OF SPORTS OR ACTIVE LEISURE ACTIVITIES TO PLAN & DELIVER AN ACTIVITY

Good sports leaders have the character and motivation to produce winners. They have also developed a range of leadership skills to help them achieve this goal. Good sports leaders need strong communication and organisational skills.

Sports teams cannot succeed without leaders. Without leaders, there is no-one to drive a team forward to achieve. A strong leader can motivate a team to achieve feats that players might only imagine in their dreams.

Have you got what it takes to succeed as a sports leader?

In this unit you will learn:

- About the qualities and responsibilities of someone who is supporting a sport or active leisure leader
- About the different parts of a sports or active leisure session
- How to help plan for an activity
- How to help deliver part of an activity

Why is planning before delivering an activity important?

L01 What qualities do you need?

Leaders of sports or leisure activity sessions need to have a range of **qualities** to be effective.

Being a role model

To be a leader, you need to be able to manage responsibility. The way you act should offer a positive role model to others. This means setting a good example by showing the right attitude, being correctly dressed and using appropriate language at all times. Sports and active leisure leaders need to be aware of their responsibilities under law towards young people. They need to be informed about and actively consider health and safety issues. They must treat everyone equally and fairly whatever their background.

Appearance

A professional appearance is important to being a positive role model. It is important that a leader is smart, clean and wears suitable clothing for the activity they are taking or have organised.

Being motivated and motivating others

People who are motivated keep the reasons why they are taking part clearly in focus at all times. What motivates a person relates to the reasons for their positive attitude or why they do what they do.

Good leaders are focused about what they are doing and why. They also need to know what motivates others.

There are two forms of motivation – *intrinsic* and *extrinsic*. Intrinsic motivation relates to the reasons why you act in a particular way and comes from within you. A long-term ambition or desire to achieve a particular goal or target is an example of an intrinsic motivation. Extrinsic motivation relates to factors 'outside' you. The admiration of friends and family, or winning medals and trophies are examples of extrinsic motivations. Knowing what motivates participants is important to the success of the activity they are taking part in and the enjoyment that they gain from it.

Key term

Qualities
A person's positive features.

Personality
What makes you who you are.

Activity: What motivates you?

Discuss with a partner what motivates you in sport or active leisure. Are your motives the same or different?

Good communication

Leaders communicate clearly. This means speaking clearly, keeping instructions simple and using words participants understand. You may need to explain things more than once. Giving clear instructions is vital to the success of an activity. Participants that receive clear instructions will feel more confident about the activity they are taking part in. Clear communication also helps prevent accidents.

Personality and style of leadership

Personality is important. Different personalities produce different types of leader. Some styles of leadership are more suited to certain activities. For the purpose of leading a particular activity, we can learn to take on a different style than that which comes to us naturally.

An *autocratic* leader leads from the front and makes all the decisions. This is important when an event involves large numbers, young children, beginners or a dangerous activity. A *democratic* leader involves participants in making decisions and is often used with older participants.

Whatever your personality and natural style of leadership, you must be enthusiastic, friendly, motivating and confident.

Functional skills

Practise good communication when discussing issues in lessons. This will help you develop your skills in **English**.

Case study:

Sir Alex Ferguson

Sir Alex Ferguson is one of the most successful football team managers. Sir Alex managed Aberdeen in the early to mid 1980s, before going to Manchester United in 1986. He has been manager of the team ever since and is the longest serving manager of any of the current Premier League teams. He has won the Manager of the Year award the most times in British football history for his outstanding management of the team.

Activity: The qualities of a leader

With a partner, think about the qualities that have helped to make Sir Alex Ferguson so successful.

Explain why each quality is important.

✔ Check

- Leaders need a range of qualities to be good leaders
- They must be motivated and enthusiastic
- They must show initiative and be good communicators.

L01 What responsibilities will you have?

Certain **responsibilities** are involved in assisting a leader with an activity.

Professional conduct

When working with young people, professional conduct is important. This means that a leader must not take advantage of their position of leadership, but rather be a role model at all times. When working with children, you must:

- Use appropriate language
- Avoid the wrong kind of contact
- Set a good example.

Key term

Responsibilities
Things you have to do as part of your job.

Activity: Poor role models

Think about a recent sports event you have been to or seen on TV where sports professionals behaved badly. It may have been a rugby match during which players were clearly swearing or fighting with each other. Think about the effect this could have on young people watching the event. If you had to tell the sports professionals responsible why their actions were inappropriate what would you say?

Health and safety

The health and safety of everyone taking part in any sport or active leisure event is most important. At a basic level, everyone should do a warm up and cool down properly to avoid injuries. Before any event, a **risk assessment** must be completed to work out any potential hazards and take steps to reduce risk.

Key term

Risk assessment
A process for identifying hazards and risks to people.

! Remember

- There are health and safety laws that are everybody's responsibility at work today. This means you must carry out the responsibilities that apply to you properly at all times.

Activity: Your responsibilities at an event

Choose an activity you would like to assist with. Draw up a list of the different responsibilities you would have as an assistant if you were helping with this activity.

Insurance

Any sport or active leisure event will require insurance to be arranged by the event organiser. This is to protect not only participants, but also spectators, local residents and leaders themselves, against the possibility of an accident.

Activity: Helping at a hockey match

Image you are helping out at a local hockey match. What kinds of risks and dangers do you think you might find there? What steps would you take as an assistant to deal with them?

✔ Check

- You must behave appropriately around children at all times
- Pay careful attention to health and safety rules and guidelines.

L01 Legal matters

There are certain legal matters that need to be thought about and acted upon when leading an event.

Child protection

All leaders and staff working with young people must have a current CRB check to show that there is no reason why they should not be working with young children.

CRB stands for Criminal Records Bureau. A CRB check is carried out to make sure that people who will have close contact with children have not committed any offences against children in the past and so are safe to work with them.

In addition activities designed for children must meet current Child Protection laws.

There are a range of other legal responsibilities that relate to sport and active leisure events. Activities must have the correct staff to learner ratio. This is the number of participants that one member of staff can supervise. For instance, a canoe instructor may have only ten participants in a group. If an accident happened and there were more participants than this, there would be serious legal consequences.

Activity: Staff to pupil ratio

You have been asked to assist with a sport or active leisure activity. You can decide what the activity is. Find out if there is a recommended staff to pupil ratio. How many staff would you need to manage a class of 20 children? What equipment would you need to deliver the activity safely?

Equality

It is important that facilities are open to all who wish to participate and do not discriminate against any one individual or group. Unless an activity is specifically designed as an activity for children of a certain age, or for older people, for example, any person, regardless of their age, gender, ethnic background or disability must be able to participate. Any form of discrimination is against the law.

Activity: Promoting equality

Talk to a partner about steps you could take to make sure that the activity you are planning is open to anyone who wants to participate.

Check

- All leaders and staff working with young children must have a current CRB check

- All activities must have the correct staff to learner ratio

- Activities should be open to all who wish to participate.

L01 Ethics & values

When any event takes place, it needs to follow a set of agreed ethics that respect certain values.

Ethics are the rules or standards for how people should behave. Values are concerned with the things that are important to people and which they regard as good or worthwhile in their own right. Equality is an example of an important value that is good for everybody. In terms of ethics, it follows that we should try to include everybody and be tolerant of people who are different from us.

In sport, it is important that activities promote good behaviour, that players follow the rules and that activities include all who wish to take part. It is important that leaders act as good role models and treat people the way they would want to be treated.

The table gives examples of different ethics and values in practice.

Type of event	Ethic or value	Example that might be seen
Basketball tournament	Fair play	Referees applying the rules at all times
Camping activity	Respect	Making sure no litter is left behind
School sports day	Safety	Checking the area to be used before use
Netball tournament	Integrity	Coaches not encouraging players to pretend to be injured

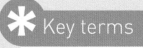

Key terms

Ethics
General rules for how people should and shouldn't behave.

Values
The things that are important to people.

Case study:

Netball tournament

Danielle is assisting at a school under-12s netball tournament, where 12 teams are competing for a regional award. While she is assisting, she notices that one of the coaches is constantly questioning the umpires in front of his team. The coach makes comments out loud whenever an umpire makes a decision that goes against his team. Towards the end of the event, Danielle notices that the coach's players are starting to copy him.

Later, during a close match, the same coach starts to shout very loudly at his own goal shooter who is having a bad game and has missed several shots on goal. Eventually, the player becomes really upset, starts to cry and is then taken off by the coach who tells them, so everyone can hear, that they are 'useless'.

Activity: Poor ethics

What examples can you find of poor ethics by this coach? Why is this type of behaviour not acceptable?

Check

- Ethics are the rules or standards for how people should behave
- Values are the things that are important to people and which they regard as good or worthwhile in their own right.

L02 What makes a sports or active leisure session?

Any sport or active leisure activity should consist of the following:

- A warm up
- The main body of the activity
- A cool down
- Feedback.

Warm up

All sports and leisure activities should start with a warm up. The purpose of a warm up is to raise both pulse and body temperature and to mobilise joints and stretch muscles. Any activity which gradually raises both pulse rate and body temperature could be used. A warm up helps to reduce the risk of injury to participants. If you are taking a warm up, try to make it fun, especially for children.

Main body

It is during the main body of the activity that skills are taught or technical development takes place. In a team activity, the activity leader might assist with tactical or fitness development. The main body of an activity should provide an opportunity to practise any skills being taught in a game situation. You should include a range of practice exercises and drills to allow all participants to progress.

Cool down

The cool down follows the main body of the session and is designed to gradually reduce both pulse rate and body temperature, as well as to remove waste products from the system to reduce soreness and stiffness. A cool down might involve jogging, gradually slowing to a walk, followed by *static* stretching exercises to finish.

Feedback

It is important for participants to receive feedback on their performance from leaders after the event. Participants can give feedback to the event organisers about their performance as well as about the event itself.

Feedback may be given and received verbally or in writing. It is best gained either at the end of the event or soon after the event. Feedback to participants should be given as soon as possible to be of value.

Feedback is designed to identify where improvement needs to be made. As a sports or active leisure leader, your feedback about how participants are performing a skill they are learning should enable them to perform the skill more successfully.

Activity: An outline session plan

Plan a sports or active leisure session in outline. Include details in your plan under each of the above headings. In pairs, explain to a partner each stage of your sports or active leisure activity, as if your partner was going to be assisting you with the session.

✔ Check

- An activity should include a warm up, main body, a cool down and feedback

- The warm up helps to prevent injury and the cool down helps reduce soreness after the event

- Feedback helps participants to improve and helps you to be a better leader or assistant.

L03 Planning a sports or active leisure session

If you are going to lead or assist with any sports or active leisure session you need to know details of the plan. Planning is the key factor in the success of any event or activity.

There are a number of things that need to be thought about and included in the planning of an event. The table below breaks down what needs to go into a session plan.

Area of planning	Issues to think about
Location	Where will the event be held? Will transport be needed? Do we need a booking facility?
Health and safety	Has a risk assessment been done? What about First Aid provision? Is security an issue? What about insurance?
Equipment	What equipment will we need? Do we have what we need or will we need to buy more?
Outcome	What is the purpose of the event? What are we hoping to achieve? (eg charity fundraiser, health awareness, sign up more members, etc)
Participants	Who is participating? How many participants are we planning for? How old are they?
Warm up	What activities would be best to prepare for the main body of the session?
Main body	Is it going to be a skills-based session or a fitness session? Will we be teaching tactical skills or technical?
Cool down	What activities would be good for the cool down?
Feedback	Who needs feedback and why? What type of feedback is needed?

Activity: Make a detailed session plan

Building on the work you did on an outline session plan for the last activity, make a more detailed session plan, including the details covered in the table above.

! Remember

Planning takes time. Allow enough time to ensure that all tasks are completed. This may require meetings with others, writing letters, booking facilities and so on.

Activity: Group discussion

It is often said that 'if you fail to plan, you plan to fail'. What do you think this means?

Case study:

The wrong plan

Matthew is organising a sports class for a group of teenagers and uses a session plan prepared for another class. The warm up and main body of the session look like this:

Activity		Basketball			
Number of participants	12	Lesson objective	To introduce chest passing to participants		
Time allowed	Content	Learner activity		Equipment required	Assessment of Learning
5-10 mins	Warm up	Pulse raiser: a game of 'Stick in the Mud' Dynamic stretching: lunges, high knees, and heel flicks		None	Observe participants
15 mins	Passing	1. Chest pass in pairs 2. Passing relays in threes		6 balls & bibs 12 cones	Observe participants Ask questions
20 mins	Basketball game	1. Bench ball games: three on three 2. Small 'Round Robin' tournament		2 balls 4 benches 6 bibs stop watch	Observe use of chest pass No dribbling allowed Chest passes only

Activity: Planning for your participants

In small groups discuss the choice of activities included in the warm up and the main body of the session. Are they suitable for teenagers?

What other details would you expect to find in the rest of the plan that have been missed out above?

Remember

The type of participants affects the type of activities you should choose.

Check

- Planning takes time and requires careful thought
- You should plan with your participants in mind
- The activities you select will affect your choice of equipment, the session plan and what you need to do to review the activity.

L04 Supporting the delivery of a sports or active leisure session

When you help a session leader, coach or tutor deliver an activity you might be asked to provide help or be responsible for one particular area – the warm up or the cool down, for example. You might be asked to take a small number of the participants and assist in the delivery of a skill development activity.

You will need to show certain skills and qualities and take on certain responsibilities when assisting. Here are some ways you might be involved:

- Taking the warm up
- Helping to select activities
- Taking an activity in the main body of the session.
- Taking the cool down
- Giving feedback

Giving a skills demonstration

You may help at an event by demonstrating a skill. Giving a demonstration is itself an important skill when you are coaching.

- You must make sure that you get your demonstration right, or instead beginners will learn how *not* to do it
- Your demonstration must also be clearly explained, so that participants know what to do.

Assistant's checklist

Whatever you are assisting with, you need to demonstrate the following skills and qualities:

- You need to be *enthusiastic* with participants
- You need to be able to *motivate others* – this means keeping yourself and participants focused on the goal and encourage them forwards
- You need to *choose activities that are suitable for participants*
- You should be *suitably dressed*.

You also need to *show responsibility for health and safety*:

- Checking the area to be used
- Looking out for any illnesses or injuries
- Thinking about the clothing and footwear of the participants
- Explaining the 'ground rules' to participants.

You can use this table to help you remember what you need to do:

Safety		
1.	Has the pitch been checked?	☐
2.	Right equipment for age group?	☐
3.	Are participants suitably dressed?	☐
4.	Anyone wearing jewellery?	☐
Activities		
1.	Warm up completed?	☐
2.	Cool down completed?	☐
3.	Are drills and practices safe?	☐
4.	Correct staff–learner ratio?	☐
Ground rules		
1.	Explained to participants?	☐
2.	Checked participants understand?	☐
3.	Are participants keeping the rules?	☐
4.	Action taken against rule breakers?	☐

Activity: Assisting with an activity

Think of a sport or active leisure activity you do that you could assist with. Keep a notebook recording how you supported the leader before, during and/or after the activity. Ask the activity leader to write a witness statement describing and commenting on your help. You can include this statement as evidence towards meeting the assessment criteria.

Check

- When giving a demonstration, get it right and provide a clear explanation

- Whatever you do to support delivery of an activity, be positive, encourage and motivate participants

- Plan your activity carefully, know your plan and think safety.

ASSESSMENT OVERVIEW

While working through this unit, you will have prepared for completing the following assessment tasks:

○	1.1	Describe the qualities needed to support a sports or active leisure leader including: • personality • motivation • communication skills	Pages 98–99
○	1.2	Identify the responsibilities when supporting a sports or active leisure leader including: • professional conduct • health and safety	Pages 100–105
○	2.1	Suggest what would be included in the plan for a sports or active leisure activity	Pages 106–107
○	3.1	Contribute to a plan for an activity for part of a sports or active leisure activity	Pages 108–109
○	4.1	Help to deliver an activity according to an agreed plan, demonstrating: • your communication skills • professional conduct • awareness of health and safety	Pages 110–111

edexcel

Assignment tips

- Watch a sport or active leisure session and identify the qualities used by the leader

- Try to identify the different parts of the session and what is involved at each stage

- Try to identify and note what the leader and any assistants are responsible for

- Plan well for any part of a session you are involved with and know your plan

- When assisting, have your plan close by in case you need to remind yourself of what you are doing.

WORKING IN SPORT & ACTIVE LEISURE

There are a number of skills you will need to develop if you are going to work in the sport and active leisure industry. Your personal presentation is important and you must have good communication skills. You must show good customer service and act as a member of a team. If you work in sport and active leisure you should expect to work shifts, rather than 9 to 5.

In this unit you will learn:

- How to show good customer service

- How to work as a team member in sport and active leisure

- About work patterns and how to manage your time

Why is good customer service so important to sport and active leisure employers?

L01 Your personal presentation

Looking the part is important to both the organisation you work for and its customers. Many organisations have a set uniform and standard of dress so that employees are easy for customers to recognise. For example, lifeguards worldwide wear a red and yellow uniform so that holidaymakers from other countries will recognise them if they need help.

It is important that you take care of your personal hygiene and that you are clean and tidy. Do you have clean hair, hands and finger nails? Is your breath fresh? Do you use deodorant regularly? Failure to wash your body and clothes properly leads to a build-up of dirt and bacteria, which causes nasty smells to develop.

If your appearance and hygiene are poor:

- You present a poor image of yourself and the organisation that employs you to customers

- You increase the risk of health problems. For example, if you handle food, dirty hands and nails may spread illness.

- People will be put off from working with you.

Activity: Checking your personal hygiene

Indicate on a copy of the body outline below, all the places where you need to take care of your personal hygiene. Describe what actions you should take and what problems might follow if you do not take enough care.

Check

Your personal hygiene is important because:

- It gives a positive impression

- It prevents you from giving offence to others

- It reduces the risk of the spread of infection and illness.

L01 Communication skills

If you work in sport or active leisure you will have regular contact with customers and other employees. You will need to be a good communicator.

The two main ways people communicate are verbally and non-verbally. Verbal communication involves speaking and listening to people. We tend to think these are the most important communication skills, but:

- Only 8% of communication comes from words that are *actually spoken*

- 42% of the message comes from the *tone of voice* – the way in which the words are spoken

- A full 50% is conveyed through *facial expression and body language.*

Most of the meaning of what you say comes from *how you say things* and *how you look* when you are speaking. At work you should always be polite and friendly, speak *clearly* and show confidence in your body language.

Non-verbal communication

Non-verbal communication includes what we communicate with our eyes, the gestures we use and the way we hold our body (our *posture*).

Making eye contact

When communicating, it is important to make eye contact. Making eye contact means you are interested and are focused on what is being said.

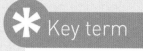

✳ Key term

Communication
The giving and receiving of information.

Functional skills

Practising your speaking and listening skills with others will help you develop your skills in English.

Activity: Pair work

How you would feel if someone you were talking to was not looking at you? What would you think about them if they were:

- Looking over your shoulder at someone else?

- Looking at their feet?

- Looking around constantly?

Activity: 'Reading' body language

Look at the image of the security man below. What do you think his body language is saying?

Standing with your hands on your hips, or your arms crossed, often is meant to signal that you are ready for what is coming next and will not stand for any nonsense. It is an *assertive* body posture. This is generally not the right way to approach a customer. You need to be aware also that wearing a uniform presents you as one of the people in charge. Be friendly and adopt an open, non-threatening body posture.

Check

- Sport and active leisure is about working with people so you need to be a good communicator by speaking clearly and listening carefully
- We communicate both verbally and non-verbally
- How we speak, our faces, what we do with our eyes, and the way we hold our body communicate strong messages.

L01 The importance of good customer service

Customer service is about giving customers the goods and service they require in a way that meets their expectations.

Good customer service is especially important to sport and active leisure organisations because they depend on *repeat business*. This means they depend on customers returning again and again. It means they have to put effort into satisfying and developing a relationship with their customers.

Activity: Group discussion

Think about a sport or active leisure centre you know. What would it be like if people only ever went once? What would be the consequences for the way the centre is run?

If you give every customer the very best service possible at all times, they will be much more likely to come again and to bring their friends as well.

Meeting expectations

Customers will be satisfied and return to your centre if they find that their *expectations* are met. A person's expectations are what they expect to happen.

Activity: Group discussion

When you go for a meal, you expect the food to be good, properly cooked and safe to eat. You also expect the waiter or waitress to be properly dressed, clean and tidy. What might a customer expect when visiting a swimming pool or health studio? What do *you* expect?

Have you ever had the experience of *your* expectations of a sport or active leisure facility not being met? How did you feel?

Happy customers = happy staff

The diagram shows how good customer service works in an organisation's favour.

When customers' expectations are met, they come back and they tell their friends.

The more customers that use the services and facilities offered at a centre, the more successful its business will be.

Satisfied customers say thank you, give praise and complain less. This makes staff feel good and gives you *job satisfaction*, which means you enjoy your job more. As a result you will work harder and perform better, making the centre even more successful.

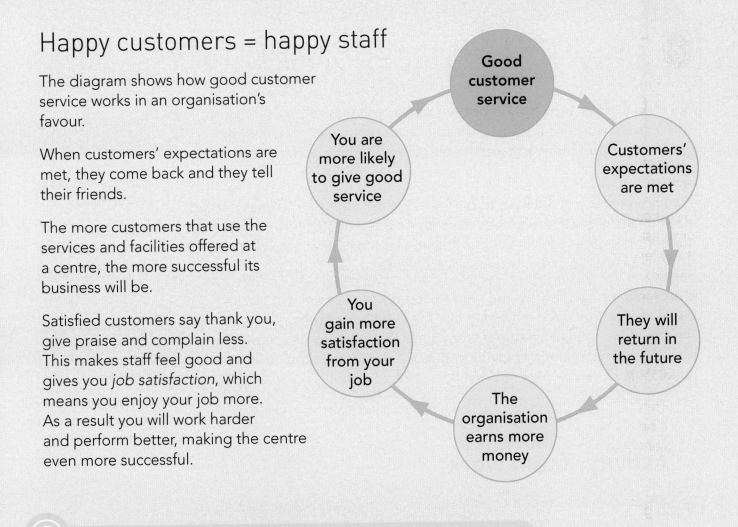

Activity: Staff room poster

Make a poster to display in a sport or active leisure centre staff room. Your poster should explain why good customer service is important. Use appropriate images and examples to help you explain.

Check

- Sport and active leisure depends on *repeat business* so all staff have a responsibility to give good customer service

- Customers will return if their *expectations* are met, meaning greater *job satisfaction* for staff

- If you are happy in your job, you will work harder and the company you work for will do well.

ⓛ02 Working as a team member

We have already seen how important good communication is in sport and active leisure. You need to be able to communicate clearly with customers. You also need to communicate well when working as part of a team.

A common task you will have to perform as a member of a team is putting up and taking down equipment. In order for a team to work well together, it is important that each individual follows manufacturers' guidelines and safety procedures correctly to avoid accidents.

Manufacturers' guidelines give step by step instructions about how a piece of equipment should be set up. The Health and Safety at Work Act lays down the law on safety procedures that need to be followed at work. Your employer may provide you with additional guidance in a staff handbook.

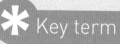

✳ Key term

Guidelines
A step by step set of instructions.

Procedures
The way something should be done.

Functional skills

Reading guidelines will help you improve your reading and develop your skills in English.

Activity: Team work

In teams, choose a sport or active leisure activity that involves the use of some specialist equipment. Find out if there are any guidelines or procedures you should follow. Practise setting up and taking down the equipment together before demonstrating for your tutor and the rest of your class.

Activity: Trampoline club

Sam is a member of a team of staff who have been asked to set up a trampoline for a club training session. Sam must work with the team to make sure the job is done efficiently and safely.

The instructor gathers the team to give them their instructions. Sam and the team then discuss the task briefly together to make sure that everyone knows what they are doing, when to do it and how. He has to:

1. *Listen to instructions.*
2. *Ask when he is unsure.*

Sam needs to work as part of a team to lift and transport the equipment. He suggests different things the team could try to make moving the equipment easier. He cooperates with the rest of the team to ensure the task is carried out safely and efficiently.

Sam shows respect to the instructor because he is in charge of the activity and knows the skills that are needed to use the trampoline safely.

Functional skills

Being able to listen will help you develop your skills in English.

Activity: Group discussion

What other qualities do you think you need to work well in a team?

Storing equipment safely

All equipment needs to be stored properly after use, so that it is not stolen, lost, misused or damaged, and to make sure that it does not cause injury. Every item of equipment should have a set place where it is stored. Equipment storage areas should be secure to prevent people who should not have access to the equipment from using it.

✓ Check

- You need to communicate clearly when working as part of a team
- Listen carefully, follow any procedures and guidelines provided, and ask questions if you do not understand
- Store all equipment safely after use.

L03 A typical working day

The sport and active leisure industry provides people with opportunities to participate in different activities in their spare time. Most people's leisure time is before 9 or after 5 when they are not working. In order to attract and provide for as many people as possible, centres need to be open long hours every day, seven days a week.

Working shifts

This will means that you will most likely work on a shift system. A shift system splits the day into different work periods, often called 'earlies' and 'lates'. Each shift has its own team of staff. The law limits how many hours you can work in a week, so centres need lots of staff to make sure that they can stay open, for example from 6 am to 11 pm every day.

You will find that one week you may be on an early shift, which means starting at 6 am and finishing at 2 pm and the next week you may be on the later shift starting at 2 pm and finishing at 10 pm. Teams will rotate on a weekly basis. Some weeks you will start and finish early in the day, but the next week, you will start and finish later. Some centres even have shifts that require staff to work 'nights'. For example, staff at a youth hostel will require some staff to be on duty during the night in case of any incidents.

Weekends and holidays

The nature of sport and active leisure means you might also have to work weekends or even bank holidays.

As with any other job, you will receive annual leave. You are entitled to a minimum of 5.6 weeks paid annual leave. This amounts to 28 days for someone who works a five-day week.

Activity: Full- or part-time?

Choose someone you know who works full-time and someone who works part-time. Find out from them what their hours of work and holiday entitlements are and how these are worked out.

Activity: Interview with a shift worker

Ask your tutor to invite people working in sport and active leisure who work shifts to come to class to speak to you. What do they think about working a shift system? What are the advantages and disadvantages of shift work for them? How do they cope with the changes to their working day when their shift changes?

Check

- Shift work involves early starts and finishes, but also late starts and finishes

- You will alternate between the two

- You will probably be asked to work weekends and bank holidays.

L03 Getting ready for work

Starting work in sport and active leisure will mean big changes for you. As we have seen, you will have to work a shift system, which means your start and finish times will change each week. You will need to learn to plan for your shift and organise yourself so you are ready for it. This involves learning to use and manage your time well.

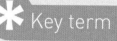

Key term

Time management
Using your time effectively so you are not late for work and all tasks are completed on time.

Getting organised

First, you must get ready for work. This will involve organising:

- What you are going to wear

- How you are going to get to and from work

- Any equipment you need to take with you

- A budget, so that you have money for travel, lunches and so on.

Getting ready for work each day will mean you need to get up in time to get washed and dressed, eat breakfast and travel to work so you arrive in time to start your shift. You may decide to get your work clothes out ready and prepare your lunch the night before.

Allowing time for travel

Where your job is will tell you how much time you need to allow for travelling. Remember, the time your shift starts will affect how much time you need to allow for travel as traffic may be heavier at different times and bus or train times may vary. How far you travel and how you travel will affect the cost of getting to and from work. If you travel by car it may be quicker, but you will need to allow for the possibility of bad traffic.

! Remember

Allow plenty of time for unexpected problems on your way to work.

Activity: Starting a new job

Imagine that you had got a job at a local sport or active leisure centre. Make a list of what you would need to organise to be prepared for starting work.

Find out how long it would take you to get to and from work for different shifts. What do you think the best way of travelling would be and why?

Check

- Starting work requires you to be organised and to manage your time well

- You need to think about what you wear and any equipment you may need

- You may need to get ready the night before to make sure you are on time.

ASSESSMENT OVERVIEW

While working through this unit, you will have prepared for completing the following assessment tasks:

○	1.1 Describe good customer service	Pages 118–119
○	1.2 Demonstrate communication skills when dealing with customers	Pages 116–117
○	2.1 Work as a team member to set up the equipment for a sport or active leisure activity	Pages 120–121
○	2.2 Work as a team member to take down the equipment from a sport or active leisure activity	Pages 120–121
○	3.1 Help identify the different shift patterns for two people working in sport and active leisure	Pages 122–123
○	3.2 Describe how to manage your time effectively when working shift patterns in sport and active leisure	Pages 124–125

edexcel

Assignment tips

- Think about what you expect when you visit a sport or active leisure facility

- Practice communication skills as often as possible

- Plan how you are going to put up and take down equipment *before you start*

- Agree what you will do with your team

- Look at a range of sport and active leisure facilities to understand what is involved in working different shifts.

SPORT & ACTIVE LEISURE GROUP PROJECT

To work in sport and active leisure you need to be able to work well with others in a team. This unit provides the opportunity for you to practise and develop those skills as you work with others on a group project. Working in a small group in this way, you will be able to develop the skills you will need when you start work.

In this unit you will learn:

- How to research an aspect of sport and active leisure

- How to present information as a team member

- To look at how well you have done with your research and say what could be improved

Why is it important to be realistic about your own strengths and weaknesses when working in a group?

L01 What are you going to research?

For your project you will be doing research to find out information about an aspect of sport and active leisure. There are many areas of sport and active leisure that you could choose to look at for this project.

The two main areas that you might choose to find out something about are facilities and events.

Facilities

Facilities include all the purpose-built and natural locations where sport and active leisure takes place. Your group project might involve finding out information about:

A purpose-built facility, such as:

- A sports hall
- A fitness facility
- A pitch or playing field.

A natural facility, such as:

- A park
- A lake
- A river.

Alternatively, you might decide to look at how good sport and active leisure is in your area in one particular sport, or even in general. For example, how many football pitches are there in your town compared with other areas? How many different fitness classes are organised for men, women or that are open to both? How good is provision for cycling? Are there enough cycle routes through the town?

Events

You might consider comparing different local charity events that have been organised and how successful they have been. How much money did each raise?

You might look at the need to improve provision for a particular activity, age group or in a particular area. You may be able to work with a local centre to find out whether there is an activity that customers would like to see offered that they have not yet tried.

Research projects can be very useful. A lot of research had to be done for the London 2012 Olympic bid to see if the city could manage the event. This project took a great deal of time, money and effort to complete.

Activity: Small group planning

In small groups, discuss your ideas for a project and think about the strengths and weaknesses of each idea, how useful the research would be, and how much work would be required.

Functional skills

Discussing your ideas will help you develop your skills in English.

Checking

- Your project can focus on any aspect of sport and active leisure
- It might focus on a particular facility or event.

🔵L01 Carrying out research

Whatever you decide to look at for your project, you need to think about how to collect the information or **evidence** you need. There are many sources you can use.

Research on the internet

Internet search engines such as Google or Bing are very good for finding information about many subjects but are not always so good for finding information about local services.

Questionnaires

Your group might need to get out and about to ask people what they think or feel. Discuss with your group what questions you need to ask to find out what you need to know. You can then write up a questionnaire and use this to gather people's views. If you use questionnaires you will probably need to fill in quite a few and collect the results to make your research meaningful. You can present the results in the form of a table or chart like the one opposite, which shows the popularity of spectator sports in the USA.

✳ Key term

Evidence
Information that shows what you say is true.

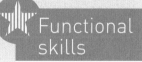

Functional skills

Researching information on the internet will help yaou develop your skills in **ICT**.

◎ Activity: Group activity

What other sources of information might be useful to find out information about facilities or events in your area?

Other sources of information

It may well be that some or all of the information you need has already been gathered by someone else. You may find that research has already been done by a local sports and active leisure centre. You may find the information you need from your local council, authority or library. It is a question of knowing who to ask. As your tutor for advice.

! Remember

Some information must be kept confidential. This means you need to keep it secret. For example, you might need to protect the personal details of a person who gave information, or make sure that only certain people have access to that information.

Activity: Practice questionnaire

Design a simple questionnaire to find out the popularity of various sports in your class. Which sport do most people play? Show the results of your research in a simple table or graph like the one below, which shows the popularity of spectator sports in the USA.

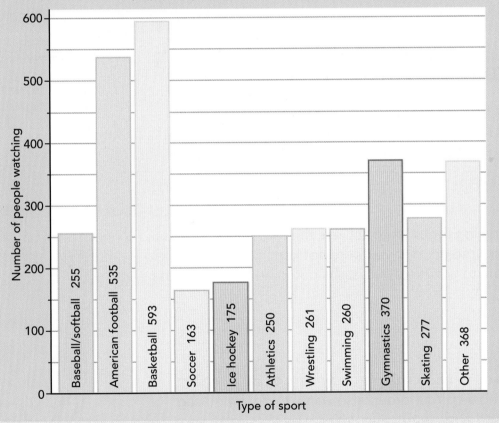

✓ Checking

- There are several different ways to carry out research so choose the sources that best match your project
- It is a good idea to use a range of information sources in your project
- Remember that some information may need to be kept confidential.

L01 The importance of teamwork

To succeed in your project, you need to work as members of a team. This means that you must all help each other. Just like in a football team, everyone has a job to do, from the goalkeeper to the centre forward.

You can show your teamwork in a number of ways. When you discuss ideas for your project, you can contribute suggestions of your own. When you come to make a plan, you might suggest to the group ways of getting the information you need. You also need to be prepared to listen to other people's ideas too.

Working in a team will require you to develop a number of teamwork skills.

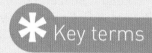 **Key terms**

Teamwork
Working together, not separately.

Negotiation (negotiating)
Reaching an agreement through talking.

Activity: Group discussion

How many different teamworking skills and qualities can you think of? Which do you think are the most important?

Cooperation

Cooperation means working together to achieve the same aims. Your group might decide on a project that you were not keen on. However you must now cooperate to achieve a successful outcome so you all pass this unit.

Negotiation

Sometimes, you will need to *negotiate*. You may want to do a certain job which another member of your group also wants to do. By talking through this problem and negotiating, you should be able to agree a good outcome. This might involve you sharing responsibility for a task, or trading places for a particular aspect of the research. This is what working together is all about.

Persuasion

If you have an idea you really believe is right, then it may be important that you try to persuade the rest of the group. This means giving them solid reasons why you believe it's the right thing to do. It is important that when you try to persuade people that your view is right, you also take the time to listen to their ideas and allow time for discussion so that everyone can agree.

! Remember

Always respect what others have done. You may feel things should have been done differently but not all decisions can be made by you and you need to accept and value what other members of the group have contributed.

Activity: Self-assessment

What do you think your most developed teamworking skill is? What is your least developed skill?

Activity: Small group work

Your team has been shipwrecked and stranded on a desert island. Each member of your team must decide on one thing to bring with them from the ship before it sinks. Each member of the team must share what they have brought and explain why. As a group discuss:

• How each object could help the group survive on the island

• How they could be used together to make another useful object.

Checking

• Teamwork will be the key to your success in this unit

• In a team you need to contribute, cooperate, negotiate and persuade

• All members of a team need to respect each other at all times.

(L02) The importance of good communication

Good communication is important if you are to work well together as a group. You will need to communicate both verbally, by speaking and discussing, etc, as well as in writing. As a group, you should hold regular meetings to talk about the progress you are making and to plan your next steps. Problems may have arisen that you need to solve together.

Keeping records

As a group, keep a written record of every meeting you have during the project. Who said what? What was agreed? When did you agree each task should be completed?

Whoever keeps the written record must write clearly so that everyone can read and understand the record. Records of meetings should show the date and time of the meeting, who was there and what was said, and any actions agreed. Actions that you agree on need to have deadlines set for them so that you can check if they have been done and so that you can then move on to the next jobs.

Listening and questioning

In a meeting, sometimes you need to listen to others and what they have to say, even if you disagree. You show respect for others by listening quietly and not interrupting. If you are not sure about something, be ready to ask questions when they have finished to make sure that you understand. When you are listening to someone, look at the person who is talking and make eye contact with them. When you are asking questions, do not be rude or start an argument on purpose. Remember, you are a *team* and you need to work *together*.

Functional skills

Practising keeping clear written records will help you develop your writing and improve your skills in English.

Functional skills

Listening and questioning will help you improve your skills in English.

Activity: 'If I had a million pounds I would ... '

Gather into groups and discuss the following: 'If I had a million pounds, I would …' Practise listening to others, asking questions and showing respect to others in the group.

- What did you find difficult?

- Why do you think it was difficult?

- What communication skills do you need to develop further?

Activity: Tug of War

Why is team work important in a Tug of War?

Checking

- Good communication is essential for success in this unit

- You need to develop the ability to communicate clearly, both verbally and in writing, and by listening carefully to others

- Practise your communication skills whenever possible.

L02 Managing yourself & solving problems

Although you will work as a member of a team on this project, at some point you will work on your own to complete set tasks. You might work on your own to research an aspect of the project, when interviewing people, or when producing charts or tables.

You will need to develop all the following qualities and skills.

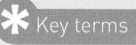

Key terms

Flexible
Able to adapt to changes or unexpected problems.

Thinking creatively
Using your imagination.

Activity: Making a plan

Make a plan of all the tasks you need to complete individually for the project you are working on at the start of each week.

Self-organisation

You need to be able to organise yourself and what you are doing in order to make sure that you complete your tasks. Planning your time, working to deadlines and being aware of what others are doing in the group, and how your work fits with theirs, will be important to your success.

Flexibility

During the project, you are likely to experience problems and delays. It is important that you can be **flexible** and change the order in which you work on different tasks. This might involve you simply changing from one task to another, or it might involve swopping roles with another group member or changing the way you had planned to do something. It is important to be flexible so that you do not waste time.

Problem-solving

Problems will arise, however good your planning is. What is important is that you deal with these problems effectively when they do arise. First you need to understand the problem. Then you can think about how to solve it. To solve problems you need to **think creatively**.

Activity: Learning to think creatively

Imagine you couldn't attend a team meeting. Think of creative ways to make sure the project does not run into problems because you were not at the meeting, and of making sure that you don't get behind on the project.

Case study:

Alex's work diary

Alex is a sports hall technician at a local college. Every day, he plans out what tasks he needs to complete. Alex looks at his online diary to see what jobs other staff have booked in that he needs to do. The online diary helps colleagues see when he is available without them having to see him in person. Once a time slot is taken up, no one else can book a job at the same time. It may be that a member of staff needs a computer and power beam setting up, or that the sports hall store needs to be tidied. Sometimes, Alex is asked at short notice to sit in on a class to assist a new lecturer or to take a register for a member of staff who is ill. In his role, he works with two different sections in the college and has to split his time between them.

Activity: Learning from Alex

1. Give examples of how Alex is managing what he has to do each day.
2. Why is it important that Alex manages his time carefully?
3. What would happen if he was unable to manage himself well?
4. What would happen if Alex was not flexible about when he did certain jobs?

✓ Checking

- You must be able to manage yourself well so that you can meet deadlines and targets
- Be flexible when you experience problems and delays
- Try to be creative in your approach to solving problems.

L03 Assessing your own work on a sport or leisure project

You will never stop learning. But if you are going to improve, you must be able to look at your performance and decide what you need to do better. This is called assessment.

There are a number of ways to assess your performance.

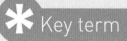

Self-assessment

Unit 11 Taking part in exercise and fitness dealt with how to assess your own performance. You can use the suggestions in that unit to assess your performance as a member of a team.

◎ Activity: Room for improvement?

Think of one area of your teamwork where there is room for improvement. Set yourself a target for this month to help you improve.

Peer assessment

You can ask the people you worked with. They might write a short report or fill out a questionnaire for you, but you could just ask them questions and write down what they say.

Line manager assessment

You could ask your tutor to comment on your performance. This would be similar to how a line manager at work might assess your performance.

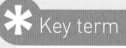

Whatever form of assessment you decide to use, it is important that it includes both your strengths – the things you did well – and your weaknesses – the areas where you need to improve in future.

Activity: Practising self-assessment

Think of an activity you have recently completed. It might be something you had to do at work, at school or college, or an activity you took part in with your sports team.

- Describe how you performed and look for areas where you could have done better

- Think about how improvement in one of these areas might improve your overall performance. For example, it might help get you a better assignment grade or perform better in your job

- Give three suggestions for how you could improve in this area.

It is important that you are open and honest in your assessment of what you did so that you can develop as a team member. Making excuses to hide behind is of no use to your development. Only if you are open and honest about both your strengths *and* your weaknesses will you become a valuable employee.

Once you have decided what needs improving, it is important to set yourself targets for the future. These targets must have a clear timeframe and they need to be realistic and achievable.

Checking

- Try to use different ways of assessing your performance to build as full a picture as possible of how you are doing

- Set targets for improvement that are realistic and achievable

- Even if you have no real weaknesses, your strengths can always be developed further.

ASSESSMENT OVERVIEW

While working through this unit, you will have prepared for completing the following assessment tasks:

○	1.1 Plan the aspect of sport and active leisure to be researched	Pages 128–129
○	1.2 Work as part of a team to research information	Pages 130–133
○	2.1 Use communication skills to present information clearly and accurately	Pages 134–135
○	2.2 Make a positive contribution as a team member	Pages 132–133
○	2.3 Use self-management skills to meet deadlines and solve problems	Pages 136–137
○	3.1 Assess your work-related skills in researching an aspect of sport and active leisure	Pages 138–139

edexcel

Assignment tips

- Try to look at more than one facility or event so that you can compare and contrast

- Use information from a variety of sources for your research

- When working as part of a team, make sure you take an *active* part and show what you can do

- Keep a *diary* or similar recording all the jobs you carried out. Get tutors or other members of the team to sign your diary to confirm what you did on the project. Ask them to comment on how well you did these jobs. Using this, then make a list of areas you need to do better and why.

JOB OPPORTUNITIES IN SPORT & ACTIVE LEISURE

At the end of this course you might want to start work in sport or active leisure. What sort of job do you think you want to do? You might want a practical, hands-on sort of job, or you might feel more at home working behind the scenes, arranging events and activities. There are lots of different jobs out there. This unit will prepare you for work in sport and active leisure.

In this unit you will learn:

- About different job opportunities in sport and active leisure

- About employment

- About the qualifications and skills you will need

- How to start a career in sport or active leisure

What job opportunities are there in sport and leisure?

L01 What jobs are there?

Activity: Who works behind the scenes?

A team is made up of many players. Here is a picture of the Chelsea Squad for 2009–10. As well as the players there are a number of other roles represented here. Who else is included in the squad? What different jobs do they do?

Different jobs

At your school or college you will find a number of different employees with roles relating to sport and active leisure. There will be PE tutors, perhaps a sports technician, maybe a sports development person (an SSCO or FESCO) to arrange activities for you.

At the sports shop in town, the sports centre or local swimming pool, your local fitness studio or gym, you will find people doing a whole variety of different sport and active leisure-related jobs.

Responsibilities

Whatever job you do you will need particular skills and abilities and you will need to be able to carry out certain responsibilities.

A *sports scientist* is responsible for providing information about a player's level of fitness.

A *sport development officer* is responsible for developing a range of activities designed to encourage people to take part in sport.

A *pool lifeguard* is responsible for supervising people in an activity.

A *manager* is responsible for running a team, selecting players and deciding the team's strategy and tactics.

Case study:

Sports leader wanted

Matt Cooper has just left school and is looking for a job in sport or active leisure. He sees a job advertised at his local centre for a sports leader. The job requires him to organise activities for children aged 11–16 during weekends and school holidays. Matthew wonders if it is worth applying.

Activity: A good fit?

What responsibilities do you think the sports leader's job will involve?

What skills will Matthew need to be able to fill the post advertised?

Check

- There are lots of different jobs in sport and active leisure
- Each job has different responsibilities
- Each job requires different skills.

L02 Employment terms & conditions

When you start a job, your job description will list certain **terms and conditions**. These have to do with:

- The job title and responsibilities
- Your hours of work
- Your wages
- The amount of paid holiday and sick pay you are entitled to
- Any pension scheme offered
- The **notice period** that must be given if you decide to leave.

Key terms

Terms and conditions
Things you have to do in return for payment for a job.

Notice period
Amount of advance warning you have to give if you want to leave a job.

Case study:
Job description

Title: Multi-sports assistant

Specific duties and responsibilities:

- To ensure the health, safety and well-being of children attending
- To maintain good customer service
- To assist in the delivery of an exciting array of sports activities
- To maintain good communications with the multi-sports leader
- To prepare and lead different sports, games and activities
- To make sure that all equipment is returned to storage neatly and in good condition.

Activity: Reading a job description

- What is the job title?
- What responsibilities are involved?
- What would you expect the hours of work to be?

Functional skills

Reading job descriptions will help you develop your skills in **English**.

Work patterns

Your work patterns have to do with when you work and for how long. Sport and active leisure facilities must provide for customers before or after their working day, so they need to be open in the evenings and at weekends. This means you will have to work in the evenings, at weekends, and even on bank holidays. Some fitness gyms are open 24 hours so you may need to work at night too.

Because you can only work a maximum of 48 hours a week, centres need large teams to keep them open for these long hours. Many people working in sport and active leisure work in *shifts* to make it possible for facilities to stay open. You might start work at 6 am one week and finish in the early afternoon. In the following week you will start later and not finish until 11 pm. As your shifts change so your work *pattern* will vary. Days off will be at weekends sometimes, but they will often be during the week.

Annual leave

Your annual leave is how much holiday you are entitled to. You are entitled to a minimum of 5.6 weeks of paid annual leave. This is 28 days for someone working five days a week. If you work part-time, you are entitled to the same level of holiday. You work it out by multiplying the length of your usual working week by 5.6. This would make 22.4 days if you only work four days a week.

Activity: Sport or active leisure centre work patterns

Visit a local sport or active leisure facility. Find out about the work patterns in operation, and why this pattern is needed for the facility visited.

Check

- Work patterns in sport and active leisure are different from other jobs
- Early starts and late finishes are part of the job
- Your work pattern will change frequently.

L02 Pay & benefits

In sport and active leisure, there are different ways that you might be paid for the work you do. The main two forms of payment are a *wage* and a *salary*. A wage is paid weekly, while a salary is paid monthly. So a wage will be shown as £X per week while a salary will be shown as £Y per year. This country currently has a minimum wage. As of 1 October 2009, the minimum wage in Britain can be broken down as follows:

- £5.80 per hour is the main rate for workers aged 22 and over

- £4.83 per hour is the rate for 18–21s

- £3.57 per hour is the rate for 16–17s (workers above the school leaving age but under 18)

- If you are of compulsory school age you are not entitled to the National Minimum Wage.

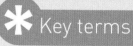

Key terms

Pay
The money you are given for the work you do.

Benefits
The 'extras' that go with a job.

Functional skills

Working out your weekly pay will help develop your skills in **mathematics**.

Activity: Calculating your wage

If you are 23 and are earning the minimum wage for a 40 hour week, what is the minimum you will earn a week?

Overtime

Your wage can be increased by working overtime. Working overtime means that you work extra hours above and beyond your normal number of hours. This might be to cover for a co-worker who is sick or to ensure that additional staff are available for a large event. Overtime hours often earn you more than your normal hourly rate. You might be paid 'double time', which means that you get twice your normal hourly rate.

! Remember

Working overtime is not a legal requirement. You may be given time off instead, paid at your normal rate.

If you are on a salary, you will not earn overtime. Your salary is fixed, whatever hours you work. Some jobs, however, provide a salary scale that you can climb up and increase what you earn. Each year, as you gain experience, you may be awarded a slight increase in your salary.

Benefits

Many jobs provide their workers with benefits as part of their employment package. For example, you may earn bonus payments for attracting new members to a gym. You may receive an annual allowance for uniforms and shoes needed for work. Your employer may provide free meals or subsidised food (which means you pay less). You may get free membership of the facility you work at. Your employer will probably send you on training and development courses to develop you as an employee.

Activity: Researching pay and benefits

In small groups, choose a sport or active leisure facility in your area. Find out about:

- The range of jobs available

- The wages or salaries paid

- The benefits that employees have available to them.

Check

- In a job, you will be paid weekly (a wage) or monthly (a salary)

- There is a minimum wage, depending on your age, that you must be paid

- Benefits are often included as part of your employment package.

L03 What skills & qualifications do you need?

You will need a range of qualifications to get a job and develop a career in sport or active leisure. A qualification is an exam, or course, that you have passed that shows you are able to do a job or activity. There are two types: essential and desirable qualifications.

A lifeguard *must* have a Pool Lifeguard qualification from the RLSS. Qualifications can be specific to a certain job or activity, or they can be more general. A football coaching award is only of use to a football coach. Your BTEC Entry 3 or Level 1 course is relevant to a range of sport and active leisure activities.

Key terms

Essential qualification
A qualification you *must* have to do a job.

Desirable qualification
A qualification an employer would like you to have if possible.

Activity: Qualifications for the job

Choose three jobs you are interested in, in sport or active leisure. List the qualifications that are essential and those that are desirable. Explain why, giving examples.

! Remember

Skills are abilities that are gained through training. Qualities are characteristics we have that make use of who we are.

Case study:

Centre duty manager

Mike is a duty manager at a large sports and leisure centre. His job is to manage the centre and staff. The centre has a sports hall, fitness suite, leisure pool, squash courts and an outdoor all weather football pitch. Mike has to meet customers, deal with suppliers and liaise with local schools that use the centre.

Today, Mike is faced with a number of problems. It is half-term and there are lots of children in the pool, but the water slide has broken down, a member of staff has called in sick and the vending machines have run out of the most popular items.

Activity: Dealing with problems

Using the table, think about what skills and qualities Michael needs to deal with the problems he is facing.

Skill or quality	Benefits of having this skill or quality	When needed?
Communication	Ensures understanding	With staff and customers
Relate to others	Keeping calm	Unhappy customer
Problem-solving	Customers kept happy	Double booking of court
Well dressed	Present correct image	When instructing in gym

Check

- You need to develop the right skills and qualities for the job you want to do

- Always try to develop the skills and qualities that you have.

L04 Getting started

Once you have decided that you want to work in sport and active leisure, how do you get started? How do you go about finding the right job for you? How do you plan for a successful career?

If you are planning a career in sport and active leisure, then you need to start by taking a close look at yourself and making some important decisions.

- What do you like doing?

- What are you interested in?

- What are you good at?

- What type of lifestyle do you want?

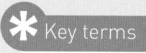

Key terms

Career
An occupation that you do for a long time.

Skills audit
An inspection of the skills you currently have and what you need to improve.

Activity: Group discussion

Why is it important to ask these kinds of questions before you start a job in sport and active leisure? What would happen if you didn't think about these things before starting?

Skills audit

The starting point in your planning for a job could be a **skills audit**.

A skills audit will help you to identify the jobs that will suit you best. Sit down and make a list of the skills you are good at and the ones that need to be improved. There are some jobs you simply aren't yet skilled or qualified enough to do. For example, if you cannot swim then being a lifeguard is not for you. To work in sport and active leisure, you need to enjoy working with people and care about giving good service. You also need to value sport and active leisure and understand why it is important to enable everyone to take part.

Lifestyle

Your lifestyle is the way in which you choose to live. What sort of lifestyle do you want? If you want your weekends to be free for playing sport, then working in sport and active leisure will conflict with this. Family or other commitments might present a barrier to you progressing in your chosen career. If you are aiming for a professional or semi-professional playing career, then working in sport and active leisure may not be for you. Changing shift patterns would conflict with your training schedule.

Activity: Setting your priorities

Make a list of ten things in your life that are important to you. At the top of your list should be something that you do not want to change or give up. As you continue with your list, add the things that are important to you, but which you might be prepared to change. Number 10 on your list should be something you are happy to change. Think about whether your priorities fit with a career in sport or active leisure.

Check

- You should start planning for your career now

- Think about all your strengths and weaknesses and look at the sort of jobs that might suit you

- Think about what is important to you and whether your priorities fit with a career in sport or active leisure.

L04 How to find a job

There are number of ways of finding the job you want. It is important to try and use them all to increase your chances of success.

Your career path

Before starting your search, it is a good idea to map the career path you see for yourself. Your career path is the series of steps that you need to take to get from where you are now to where you want to be in a few years' time. It will involve doing different jobs and probably changing employers. Your first job may not be the one you really want to do, but it may well be a first important step on the jobs ladder.

A career path might look like this, but there may be different pathways to the same end goal.

| Pool lifeguard | Senior lifeguard | Duty manager | Centre manager |

For each step you take, you will require a range of skills and experience to progress. To progress along the pathway above, you might need the following skills and experience:

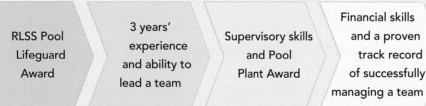

| RLSS Pool Lifeguard Award | 3 years' experience and ability to lead a team | Supervisory skills and Pool Plant Award | Financial skills and a proven track record of successfully managing a team |

Finding out about jobs

When a job becomes available, it is described as a 'vacancy' that needs to be filled. There are a number of different ways to find out about current vacancies. You can:

- Look in your local paper

- Visit a centre and ask

- Send your details to local centres

- Visit fitness centre websites

- Speak to your local Connexions career service

- Ask your friends and family.

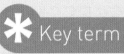

Key term

Vacancy
A job that is available.

Remember

When you start to look for a job in sport or active leisure, ask yourself the following questions:

- **What do you want to achieve in the job? Set clear, realistic goals for yourself.**

- **What will the working conditions be like?**

- **Are the hours of work right for you? Do they fit with your other commitments?**

Activity: Practice job search

Using a range of information sources, make a list of current vacancies in sport and active leisure.

Now choose a job you would like to do and send off for the details of the position. Read the job description and think about the person specification and whether you fit the profile.

Do you have the necessary skills and qualifications? What areas could you improve to make you more suitable for this kind of position?

Activity: Setting yourself a goal

Set a clear, realistic goal for yourself that you can work towards now and that will help you progress in your chosen career. Set yourself a deadline for achieving your goal.

Check

- Use a range of sources when you are searching for a job

- When you set goals for yourself, make sure you set a deadline for achieving them.

ASSESSMENT OVERVIEW

While working through this unit, you will have prepared for completing the following assessment tasks:

○	1.1	Identify jobs in different sectors of sport and active leisure	Pages 142–143
○	1.2	Describe the job roles in one sport and active leisure facility	Page 142
○	2.1	Describe the conditions of employment within sport and active leisure	Pages 144–147
○	3.1	Present information about the qualifications and skills required for selected jobs in sport and active leisure	Pages 148–149
○	4.1	Produce a plan to start work within sport and active leisure	Pages 150–153

Assignment tips

- Make a list of the types of jobs that interest you in sport and active leisure

- Make sure you know what each job involves, and what it will require of you in terms of skills and qualifications, and the roles and responsibilities that go with the job

- Make sure you understand how and when you will be paid, what your hours of work will be and what pattern your shifts will follow

- Have a career path in mind and know how to achieve each step on the way to your goal.

PHYSICAL ACTIVITIES FOR CHILDREN

Being active is important if you are going to stay healthy, both physically and mentally. It is especially important for children to be active as they grow and develop. If you want to work with children in your sport and active leisure career, you need to know what activities are right for them and how to keep them safe.

In this unit you will learn:

- About different activities for children

- What an adult has to do when working with children doing activities

- How to plan and get ready for activities for children

What do you think is important to think about when planning activities for children?

L01 Activities for children aged 0–3

Activities for children aged 0–3 years may take place inside or outside. They usually involve the use of **resources** like toys and other equipment, such as sand and paint. Children at this age are able to crawl and roll around. As they develop they will walk, run and climb. Toddlers, like the one in the photo below, enjoy pushing toys around as they learn to walk.

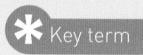
✳ Key term

Resources
Equipment and other items you use in activities.

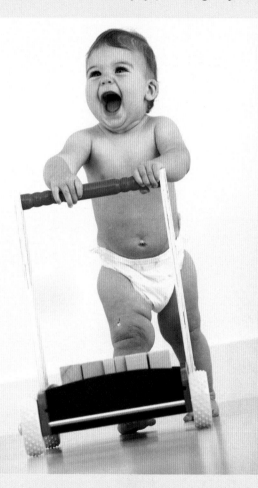

There are a number of activities you can use to help children of this age develop their physical skills. For example, you could practise bouncing, kicking or throwing a ball, or use building bricks. Music and sand both offer opportunities for encouraging young children to be active.

Activity: Group discussion

'Children amuse themselves.' Is this true? What might it mean for someone who is planning activities for children of this age?

Activity: Think about it

What do you think are the most important ingredients of a successful activity for young children?

Activity: Nursery visit

Arrange to visit a local nursery or playschool. List some of the different items of equipment you can see and activities that might make use of them.

If you are able to observe children in active play, make notes about what they are and are not able to do at this age.

Check

- Activities should be fun and interesting
- You need to allow children to try new things and give them space to practise.

L01 Activities for children aged 3–5

At this age children can be at different stages in their growth and development. For example, some children won't be able to kick a ball yet, while others will be able to do this very well.

There are a number of activities that you can try with this age group. They include:

- Hopping and skipping

- Running

- Swimming

- Balancing

- Dancing

- Digging

- Catching objects

- Using bats and other sports equipment.

You will need different resources for these activities. There are more activities that you can do with 3–5s than with 0–3s. Rather than using sand pits and building blocks, you can start to use bats and balls, hoops and ropes.

Activity: Designing an activity session

Imagine you are in charge of a class of 3–5 year olds. You have to design an activity session for them. Make a shortlist of the activities you would choose. Which do you think would be the most fun for the children? Think about what you would do to make sure the session was successful.

Here are some sports activities to try:

- Learning to swim
- Short running races
- Having a go at dribbling
- Kicking footballs at a goal
- Learning to volley a sponge ball
- Bouncing a basketball
- 'Shooting hoops' using a child-height basketball hoop.

Activity: Ideas for activities

Make a poster of ideas to show a new assistant sports leader what activities they can do with children aged 3–5.

✔ Check

- Children aged 3–5 will be able to take part in a wider range of activities than 0–3s, including sports
- You will need different resources to meet their needs.

L02 Working with children: your role

When you are working with children on an activity, whatever age they are, you will take on a variety of different **roles**.

Case study:

Swimming instructor

Chris is a newly qualified swimming instructor who teaches a range of lessons for children aged five and upwards. He teaches them each of the main swimming strokes in lessons lasting 30 minutes. He is responsible for up to ten children at a time. Before, during and after each lesson, he has a number of roles that he must carry out as an adult.

Activity: Group discussion

Think about what the children and their parents watching at the poolside expect from Chris. Discuss as a group:

1. What roles Chris has to take on

2. How Chris needs to carry out these different roles.

Key term

Role
The part a person plays in their job or the area that they are responsible for.

Supervise
Watch what someone is doing to make sure it is safe and they are doing it properly.

Chris's roles

Ahead of each lesson, Chris must make sure he has planned what he is going to do and has identified any safety hazards and assessed the risks children and adults face during his lessons. He must then take steps to deal with those hazards and minimise the risks to safety.

Before the start of each lesson, Chris must ensure that all equipment is safe and appropriate for the children to use. He must also know about the needs of each child in his group. For example, some may lack confidence in the water, while others may have a disability of some kind.

While the children are swimming, Chris will observe each child and give them advice about what they can do to improve. He will praise them to encourage them as they progress.

Chris must **supervise** the children getting in and out of the water safely so there are no accidents. He must take a register to record who is present at each lesson.

All these roles make sure that the young children are safe and have an enjoyable activity session.

Activity: Checking safety

Is the equipment in the picture safe to use?

Check

- When working with young children, you must act responsibly at all times

- You must carry out a range of roles to make sure that children are safe.

L03 Planning & preparing children's activities

When planning a children's activity session, there are a number of decisions you will need to take.

- Who is the session for?

- What activities are appropriate?

- How long is the session?

- Where and when will the session take place?

The answers to these questions will help you decide what equipment you will need. Any equipment you require needs to be the right size for the children you are planning for. It also needs to be checked for safety before the session.

If you are planning a session as a member of a team, you may need to assert yourself if you do not agree with something, or be flexible about your role if you are to work well with others. As a member of a team, you may need to take some responsibility for collecting equipment for the session, setting it up or putting it away at the end of the session.

You may need to make changes to the way you are working if feedback suggests this. For example, you may need to improve your communication skills.

✳ Key term

Assert yourself
Show confidence.

Functional skills

Listening to feedback will help you develop your skills in English.

Skills for planning and preparation

	Why?	Where needed?	Benefits
Time management	To achieve the goals of the session in the time allowed	Arriving for the session on time, keeping to the agreed schedule for the session	Achieving what has been planned for the session
Being a team member	Shares the jobs and responsibilities to make sure the job gets done	During session planning, set up of equipment, and during the session itself	Each person has an equal share of the work and can manage what they have to do
Problem-solving	Problems always arise	During session planning, set up of equipment, and during the session itself	Event will run smoothly for participants
Risk assessment for health and safety	Legal requirement	Before and during the session	Participants are safe at all times and possible accidents are prevented
Communication skills	Without good communication, you cannot achieve the aims of the session	During session planning, set up of equipment, and during the session itself	All team members clear about what the session involves and what is the goal of the session

Activity: Practise planning

In small groups plan and prepare a physical activity session for a mixed group of ten boys and girls aged 6–7. Make sure you think about all the areas in the table above.

Check

- If you fail to plan, you plan to fail! Make sure you allow enough time to plan as a team

- Make sure you know your roles and the roles others will play

- Speak up if you have a different idea, disagree, or are unable for any reason to do the job you have been asked to do.

ASSESSMENT OVERVIEW

While working through this unit, you will have prepared for completing the following assessment tasks:

◯	1.1 Describe physical activities for children 0-3, 3-5 years	Pages 156–159
◯	2.1 Explain the role of the adult when children are involved in physical activities	Pages 160–161
◯	3.1 As a team member, plan and prepare a physical activity for children and demonstrate: • self-management skills • a positive contribution as a team member • meeting agreed deadlines • problem-solving skills • safe practice • communication skills	Pages 162–163

edexcel

Assignment tips

- Talk to parents of young children about what activities their children enjoy

- If you have a younger brother or sister, watch them when they play and see what they enjoy doing

- Talk to people who work with young children about what their roles and responsibilities are while working with children

- When planning and preparing an activity for children, make sure you record in a diary or notebook how and when you have shown various skills.

EXPLORING DANCE SKILLS

Dance is an activity that has great benefits in terms of your skills and fitness. It develops your strength and flexibility, which will be important to you if you work in sport and active leisure. Learning a dance routine involves following and copying another person's moves, just like you need to be able to follow instructions at work.

In this unit you will learn:

- How to take part in dance workshops

- How to put a dance piece together and perform it

- Work skills through these activities

What does it take to be good at dance?

L01 Taking part in dance

Taking part in a successful dance routine requires certain skills and qualities. You will need a range of physical skills.

Key term

Posture
The position of your body.

Skill or quality	What is it?	What does it help with?
Good posture	Holding your body in the right position when dancing	Allows you to perform steps and moves in a routine correctly
Coordination	Being able to move parts of your body in a smooth way	Important in dance where movements need to be smooth and controlled
Balance	Steadiness when moving or standing	Helps you to complete moves confidently
Spatial awareness	Knowing where each part of your body is and what it is doing in relation to the space around you	You need to know exactly where each part of your body is in relation to other dancers and the space you are working in
Rhythm	The flow of your movements, usually to the beat of the music used in a dance	If you move off the beat the dance routine might go wrong
Timing	Your ability to perform the right moves at the right time	If your timing is not right it might throw the dance routine off beat
Interpretation	Showing what the music is saying through your movements or facial expressions	It helps make the performance more exciting and believable
Musicality	Talent in music	Helps your dance performance

Activity: Understanding different facial expressions

You will need to be able to use a range of similar expressions when dancing. What does each facial expression say to you?

Activity: Keep track of your learning

When you take part in dance workshops, keep notes on what you learn. Think about how you can show your audience the meaning of the music.

✔ Check

- Dancing requires a range of physical skills, musical ability and the ability to interpret music through facial expression and movement

- Workshops provide the chance to practise and develop these skills and abilities in a range of ways.

L02 Developing a dance performance

Choosing the music

When putting together a dance routine, the first thing you need to think about is what music you are going to use. You need to listen to different tracks to choose the one that speaks to you, and then listen to your choice again to think about what story the music tells. This is called interpretation.

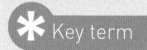

✱ Key term

Choreography
Creating a dance by putting together a dance routine.

◎ Activity: Bringing the story to life

Listen to a piece of music you like. If the music has lyrics, think about the words. What story do they tell? Once you have the story, you can then plan a dance routine that brings that story to life for the audience.

Choreography

Your tutor or instructor will design the choreography of your dance routine for you to follow. The choreography of the dance includes the steps, movements and other actions that form your routine. To follow the choreography correctly you will need to listen and watch the instructor's demonstration carefully, and then follow his/her lead as you practise to learn the right moves and steps.

Practising

When you practise a routine, there are techniques you can use to help you. *Repetition* of the steps and moves will help you remember them. Think about learning to ride a bike. When you first started, you were unsteady and made lots of mistakes, but with practice you improved until it felt completely natural. This is called *movement memory*.

The final practice is a dress rehearsal, where you perform the whole routine just as you plan to at the actual performance, but without an audience, to make sure there are no mistakes.

You may have a particular role to play in the dance. You might be a main dancer with a key part, or you may be one of the dance team. Whatever your role, you have an important part to play when you perform your dance.

Activity: Dance workshop

Imagine you are working with your instructor and the members of your group to develop a routine. What kind of attitude do you think you will need to have?

✔ Check

- Being able to understand and interpret a piece of music is important in designing a successful dance routine

- Practise as much as possible to help you learn the routine.

L03 Using dance skills in a show

In this unit you will perform a dance routine to an audience. When performing a dance it is important that your movements are just as you have practised. This involves moving your body in just the right way, by just the right amount and in the style of the music used. For example, rock and roll routines are fast and energetic. Ballet is much more expressive and formal. The **dynamic** quality of your performance is especially important.

As a dancer, you will need to focus on your movements at all times and your position in relation to the rest of the team.

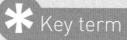

✳ Key term

Dynamic
Being energetic and lively.

! Remember

You need to use facial expressions to show the emotions you want your audience to see.

Choice of music and style

The style of your dance should be agreed with your instructor. There are many different styles to choose from. You should choose a style that fits the music and suits the talents of the group. You might choose jazz, ballet, African or even Bollywood.

Working together

The performance you give will be based on choreography designed by your instructor. It is important that you work *with* the instructor and as a team if you are to perform well.

Activity: Exploring different dance styles

Watch video clips of a range of different dance styles. Make a list of the main differences between them in movement, expression and music.

Discuss with your instructor your ideas about which styles you would like to include in your dance performance.

Activity: Performing a street dance

Think about what facial expressions you might use if you were performing a street dance routine.

Check

- There are a range of different styles that can be used for your routine

- You need to develop an understanding of music, produce accurate movements, and use a range of facial expressions

- Once you have chosen your music and talked together as a group about what style of dance your routine should follow, your routine will be choreographed by your instructor.

L04 Improving your work skills through a dance routine

As in other sport and active leisure activities, you can show you have the skills needed for work while taking part in dance.

Reliability and punctuality

Employers want staff that:

- Arrive on time
- Complete jobs when asked
- Are reliable – ie they behave like this every day.

In dance, if you turn up for rehearsals on time, with the correct clothing, and you always try your best, you will show you are reliable and punctual. These are work skills that you can practise as you prepare your dance routine.

Positive attitude

A positive attitude is important in dance and work. Smile, be enthusiastic, and be ready and willing to try new ways of performing a skill or practising a routine.

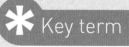
Key term

Reliability
This means you can be trusted to do something.

Punctuality
Never being late.

Activity: Dance idol?

Think of a dance performer or dance group you look up to. Which of the skills you have learned about do they have? Why do you think this makes them successful at what they do? If you were a famous dance performer how do you think these skills would help you?

Motivation

Motivated people keep the reasons why they are doing what they do in focus at all times. Be motivated! This rubs off on to others and means you will all enjoy what you are doing. Sometimes, a friend might find a particular move difficult. Helping to motivate them will keep them practising until they succeed.

Respect

Always show respect for others in the group. Remember, they may not find a move as easy to learn as you do and may need extra time or help to get it right. Instead of showing impatience or disrespect, try to help them forward.

! Remember

Always treat people how you would want to be treated by them.

You need to show respect to your instructor or dance tutor:

- Listen to what they have to say: they know more than you do

- Support other members of your dance team at all times and listen to others even if you disagree with what they say

- If you receive criticism, respond in the right way: do not lose your temper and be rude.

Activity: Keep a diary or notebook

When you are preparing for a dance routine, keep a diary or notebook of your progress. Keep a record of when you show work skills and respect for others. Ask your tutor or instructor to sign your diary.

✔ Check

- Taking part in this routine will help you demonstrate skills needed at work

- Turn up on time, be polite and respectful, enthusiastic and motivated.

ASSESSMENT OVERVIEW

While working through this unit, you will have prepared for completing the following assessment tasks:

○	1.1	Use physical skills in practical dance workshops	Pages 166–167
○	1.2	Use interpretive skills in practical dance workshops	Pages 166–167
○	2.1	Develop a dance piece with direction and guidance	Pages 168–169
○	3.1	Perform with a degree of accuracy	Pages 170–171
○	3.2	Perform using physical expression appropriate to the style of the piece	Pages 170–171
○	3.3	Perform with a degree of musicality	Pages 170–171
○	4.1	Be reliable when taking part in practical activities	Pages 172–173
○	4.2	Show a positive attitude to practical activities	Pages 172–173
○	4.3	Be respectful to others in practical activities	Pages 172–173

edexcel

Assignment tips

- Investigate a number of different dance styles to see which you like best.

- Don't be shy! Try out different styles.

- Put lots of positive effort into dance rehearsals. Try and keep a note of when you have rehearsed and how it went.

- Look out for people showing examples of good work skills. Try and show the same behaviour yourself.

- Record times when you show different work skills and respect for others. Ask a tutor or instructor to support your evidence for this unit.

Interesting facts

Unit 4: Taking part in sport

In June 2010, tennis players John Isner and Nicolas Mahut took part in world's longest-ever match. It took place over three days and ended with Isner winning 6–4, 3–6, 6–7, 7–6, 70–68.

Unit 5: Assisting at a sport or active leisure event

The modern marathon was created in honour of a Greek legend. The legend is that a Greek runner called Pheidippides ran 26 miles from a town called Marathon to the capital city, Athens, to tell the people there that the Greek army had won a battle against the Persians. After delivering his message, Pheidippides collapsed and died from exhaustion.

Unit 6: Improving own fitness

Yoga started out as a spiritual/religious practice but in the west it is often seen as a physical activity to help stay healthy.

Unit 8: Managing your health at work

A normal conversation produces about 70 decibels of noise, but a loud rock concert produces about 150 decibels of noise – which is above the pain threshold!

Unit 10: Risks and hazards in sport and active leisure

Almost one-third of the UK population has had a sporting injury at some point during their life.

Unit 11: Taking part in exercise and fitness

Over 2 million people in the UK take part in athletics (track and field, running or jogging) at least once a week.

Unit 12: How the body works

On average, a human heart beats 100,000 times a day – that's about 2.5 billion times during an average person's life time.

There are over 650 muscles in the human body.

Unit 13: Planning own fitness programme

When he was 14, Olympic diver Tom Daley was training 19 hours a week as well as going to school and doing his homework.

Unit 14: Assisting a leader of sports or active leisure activities to plan and deliver an activity

The number of people working in sport and active leisure increases by about seven per cent each summer when 'out of school' courses are run.

Unit 15: Working in sport and active leisure

In 2008, there were 5,714 gyms in the UK, according to the Fitness Industry Association.

Unit 16: Sport and active leisure group project

The planners of the 2012 London Olympics needed 70,000 volunteers to help make the games run smoothly.

Unit 17: Job opportunities in sport and active leisure

In 2004, 576,000 people worked in sport and active leisure – but there were also 5 million volunteers doing unpaid work.

Unit 18: Physical activities for children

In 2009, nearly eight out of every 10 playworkers thought that the skills needed to do the job were increasing.

Unit 19: Exploring dance skills

There are over 3,000 dance groups in the UK and they are used by more than 140,000 people in total.

Key terms

Active leisure events: Active leisure events are concerned with *non*-competitive activities, such as fun runs and charity events.

Analysis: When you talk someone through how they performed to point out what went well and what could be improved.

Appraisal: Judging how good something is.

Assert yourself: Show confidence.

Assessment: Looking at how good something is.

Attitude: Our way of thinking about something.

Barriers: Things that may prevent you from achieving the goals included in your fitness programme.

Behaviour: The way we act.

Benefits: The 'extras' that go with a job.

Body language: Movements or positions of your body that let other people know what you are thinking or feeling.

Career: An occupation that you do for a long time.

Choreography: Creating a dance by putting together a dance routine.

Communication: The giving and receiving of information.

Component: Part of something much larger. A fitness component is one part of your total fitness.

Desirable qualification: A qualification an employer would like you to have if possible.

Dynamic: Being energetic and lively.

Dynamic stretches: Stretches that involve slow, steady movement.

Emergency: A serious, unexpected situation that needs to be dealt with immediately.

Enthusiasm: Being really keen on something.

Essential qualification: A qualification you *must* have to do a job.

Ethics: General rules for how people should and shouldn't behave.

Evidence: Information that shows what you say is true.

Exercise: The activity of making use of your muscles in various ways to keep fit.

Facilities: Buildings or equipment provided for exercise and fitness.

Feedback: Information you give that shows you understand or that an agreed aim or goal has been met.

Fitness programme: A plan of activities to improve someone's fitness.

Flexible: Able to adapt to changes or unexpected problems.

Goals: Targets to aim for. They can be short-term, medium-term or long-term.

Guidelines: A step by step set of instructions.

Hazard: Anything that can cause harm.

Hydrated: How much water there is in the body.

Induction: Instruction for beginners in how to exercise and use equipment safely.

Line manager: The member of staff responsible for what you and others do at work.

Negotiation: Reaching an agreement through talking.

Notice period: Amount of advance warning you have to give if you want to leave a job.

Nutrients: What the body needs to stay healthy.

Observation: When you watch the way someone does something closely and take notes as part of a review.

Pay: The money you are given for the work you do.

Personality: What makes you who you are.

Posture: The position of your body.

Procedure: The way something should be done.

Punctuality: Never being late.

Qualities: A person's positive features.

Reliability: This means you can be trusted to do something.

Resources: Equipment and other items you use in activities.

Responsibilities: Things you have to do as part of your job.

Review: A formal assessment of something. It may be written down, allowing it to be referred to again when planning future fitness programmes.

Reviewing: Looking back on something to decide what was good and what needs improving.

Risk: The chances that an accident will happen.

Risk assessment: A process for identifying hazards and risks to people.

Role: The part a person plays in their job or the area that they are responsible for.

Rules: Tell us what we can and cannot do in sport.

Self-management: Organising yourself for an event.

Skill: An ability gained by training.

Skills audit: An inspection of the skills you currently have and what you need to improve.

Sport: An activity that involves physical exertion and competition.

Sports events: Sports events are competitive, have rules and regulations, and produce a winner.

Static stretches: Stretches done standing still.

Supervise: Watch what someone is doing to make sure it is safe and they are doing it properly.

Teamwork: Working together, not separately.

Technique: The way we perform or apply a skill.

Terms and conditions: Things you have to do in return for payment for a job.

Thinking creatively: Using your imagination.

Time management: Using your time effectively so you are not late for work and all tasks are completed on time.

Training activities: The actions that are put into a fitness programme.

Vacancy: A job that is available.

Values: The things that are important to people.

Index